Original publication: "Hudební nauka Klíček 3"
Author: Eva Šašinková, M.M., Ph.D., M.B.A.
Illustrations: Mgr. Kateřina Kovářová
Original graphic design: Lumír Kaděra
Original publisher: Czech Music Edition, Prague, Czech Republic, 2022
Website: www.hudebni-publikace.cz
Copyright: Eva Šašinková, M.M., Ph.D., M.B.A.
Original Czech version ISBN: 978-80-908706-1-1

English adaptation: "Clefi's Music Notebook 3"
Illustrations: Mgr. Kateřina Kovářová
Translation, adaptation, and graphic design: Roman Placzek, D.M.A.
Publisher: BumbleBee Notes™ Music Publishing, Manlius, NY, USA, 2025
Catalog number: cbbn002-wb-008
Website: www.bumblebeenotes.com
Copyright: BumbleBee Notes™ Inc. Music Corporation
ISBN: 979-8-9919035-7-8

Clefi's Little Crossword Review

Across:

1. A type of minor scale.
2. m3.
3. A device indicating various tempos.
4. Second, third, sixth, and seventh.
5. The primary minor scale.
10. A broad, slow tempo marking.
12. The inverted perfect fifth.
14. Cm is a chord symbol for...
15. A symbol lowering a note by two half steps.
16. A major scale with six flats.
19. The name of the song starting with m2.
20. An irregular rhythmic pattern.
21. A mode.
22 A tempo marking for speeding up.

Down:

6. Symbols used to alter primary tones.
7. A three-note subdivision of a beat.
8. P1.
9. Unison, fourth, fifth, and octave.
11. A symbol raising a note by two half steps.
13. P8.
17. "Back to the beginning."
18. A diagram for the progression of all major and minor scales..
23. D is a chord symbol for...
24. C major tonic fifth chord.

Eva Šašinková, M.M., Ph.D., MBA, the author of the series, lives in Prague, Czech Republic, where she concertizes and holds academic positions at the Pilsen Conservatory and Academy of Music in Prague. Since childhood, Eva has dreamed of becoming a music teacher, sharing her passion and experience of love for music, especially with children. She has a deep love for the double bass, her instrument, in which she holds a master's degree. However, Eva also profoundly admires the piano, an instrument that was an inseparable part of her

About the Author

childhood. This admiration is the reason behind the concept of her method, which she based on the keyboard's layout. Eva is convinced that the piano is a unique instrument designed to help explain the fundamentals of music theory, the meaning of tones and melody, and the mission of music. She successfully proves her firm conviction in the practical application of her method. The story of her project started with a children's story that came to life during a trying period in the author's life.

Her passion for teaching children and desire to share her knowledge helped her concentrate on the essentials. During her pedagogical activities, Eva noticed that the materials available to her for the curriculum presentation were not, in her professional opinion, satisfactory. She started to visit music schools in her home country, the Czech Republic, comparing, editing, reworking, and creating. As a result, Eva began to bring worksheets filled with information and fun activities to the music education classes to make students' time learning music theory more engaging, easily accessible, and entertaining. The reactions of the young music students and fellow pedagogues were overwhelmingly positive.

Professor Eva managed to engage children's senses from all angles—drawing, singing, and practical demonstrations on a keyboard—everything children appreciated. On top of that, she had "The Story of a Song, "which kicked off a star career for one little boy, Clefi. He welcomes children in his "Clefi's Little Notebook" and helps them learn more in the four volumes of his "Clefi's Music Notebook." He plays and sings with them in "Clefi's Little Music Education Notebook" (in the translated version integrated into "Clefi's Little Notebook" – editor's note) and "Clefi's Musical Instruments" written for little musicians. Clefi helps them practice their newly acquired knowledge in three workbooks full of fun tasks and exercises. Children play with little Clefi, learn, and get ready for the more dedicated encounter with Lady Music and their chosen instrument in a fun and engaging way. And maybe it will become the love of their lives, their calling, and a hobby, as it happened to the author.

And to the sad faces of those who did not have the luck to learn from the best teachers and publications and did not have the best opportunities, Eva says with her clever little smile: "If you love music and have an open heart, the muse will not ask you how old you are. She will kiss you on the brow when you least expect it. So do not wait and be ready!"

Author's Foreword

Clefi's New Music Education School
is a unified music education method for children, amateur musicians, and music students.

Based on my extensive multi-genre musical performing career, many years of experience teaching children, and my terminal education degree in music theory, I have created a unified music education program for children from an early age to young musicians who choose to study music more seriously. The New Music Education School leans on children's natural perception of music. It offers young musicians and their teachers a unified educational system of fundamental music theory aiming to support musical creativity. Its main goal is to awaken children's musicianship based on creativity and the ability to sing a song, play it on a musical instrument of their choice, and write it down correctly, the sort of musicianship that enables them to use their musical knowledge theoretically and practically.

The first book, Clefi's Little Notebook, is tailored for the youngest musicians. It introduces us to Clefi, a charming little boy who shares his story. Clefi becomes our companion on this musical adventure. In Clefi's Little Notebook, children delve into musical notation, the birth of a song, a musical note, a musical staff, a clef (which inspired Clefi's name), the musical alphabet, and a scale. They learn to read and write notes in the fourth, the middle octave, and practice their new skills through exercises, puzzles, engaging tasks, and songs they play and sing.

Clefi's Music Notebooks 1, 2, 3, and **4** follow Clefi's Little Notebook. These four full-color music textbooks stand out for their unique conceptual design. Each volume is a complete unit and can be used individually.

At the same time, all four volumes are designed as one method, seamlessly following one another, so that the children can acquire a complete knowledge of the fundamentals of music theory in a friendly and engaging way.

Beautiful illustrations and graphic design enhance the unique quality of these lovely publications. All textbooks are suitable for children, amateur musicians, and professional music students.

This music education series explains the fundamentals of music theory quickly and efficiently so that children can understand and practice them while playing musical instruments, singing, and harmonizing. The textbooks aim to develop children's musical abilities, aural skills, perception of tone pitch and duration, and rhythmical and tonal melodic structure.

The idea behind this methodological concept is to make children first listen, then understand, learn, utilize, and create. When born, a baby listens and absorbs speech. When it understands it, it tries to pronounce the first words. A child attempts to understand the connections and context. Only after several years can a child logically think and systematically create. And the same applies to the understanding of music! What would the knowledge of music theory be for if we did not listen to music and didn't use the ingenious system of music theory in practice? However, the same applies both ways. How can we expect to evolve in our music-making if we refuse to learn and explore the mysteries of music, its tonal relations, harmony, and rhythm?

This method will help children fully absorb music and learn essential human and life values through it. We can learn to read and write only if we listen to our parents talk from an early age. Then, we learn the words, pronounce them, and understand their meaning. The same applies to music and how we understand it.

I hope my books will bring you joy and help many young musicians open the door to the beautiful world of music.

Eva

What's Inside:

Similar to "Clefi's Little Notebook," this book presents a collection of enchanting folk songs from the rich Czech folklore tradition, designed for music education. To accurately utilize their intended purpose, each song requires accurate adaptation and translation into English, which would take up more space than these volumes can accommodate without disrupting their intended design. Therefore, we are offering a standalone "Clefi & Notelina's Songbook," featuring all the songs from all nine volumes of Clefi's New Music Education School series, along with accurately and sensibly translated and adapted English lyrics.

Dear musicians,

We are back to invite you once more to the world of music, a place of creativity and enchanting entertainment.

In the first Music Notebook, we began learning the basics of music theory while exploring the underwater world. In Clefi's Music Notebook 2, we completed the circle of major scales, learned more about intervals and chords, and took a journey into space together. In this part of the series, we will reach an even higher level of knowledge and enjoy even greater joy in music.

In this third part of the series, we will visit an amusement park filled with music. We will explore minor scales, which are constructed similarly to major scales. As we connect all our knowledge so far, we'll discover many new things we can now observe on our own. In the center of the park, we will spin a Ferris wheel of scales to see how they are all interconnected. Once all the parts of the wheel fit together as we connect all we know, they become balls that we can juggle with fun and ease.

Get ready for an exciting adventure with colorful balloons marking our journey! We'll dive into the captivating world of derived, upper, and lower intervals, and discover how to create magic with each one. The enchanting transformation of tones is at the heart of enharmonic exchange, and we have a unique and exhilarating learning experience ahead of us that you won't want to miss!

Let us embrace the beauty of harmony, igniting the wheels of creativity as we explore the profound functions of major and minor keys. In the journey ahead, we will find joy in the interplay of simple and combined measures, delve into the richness of compound meter, and engage in rhythmic exercises that spark our passion for music.

So, our musical friends, come to our amusement park! We look forward to seeing you there!

Yours,
Clefi and Notelina

A **SCALE** is a row of tones arranged based on specific rules. These rules primarily govern the arrangement of whole steps and half steps. In Western music, the most common scales are the **major** and **minor scales**.

A **KEY** defines the relationship between the tones of a composition and a particular scale. It has the same name as the scale it is associated with.

A **TONALITY** defines the character of a particular scale or key. Another term that describes tonality is mode. Major scales exhibit a strong, joyful, and upbeat tonality, while minor scales convey a softer, sadder, and more melancholic tonality.

MAJOR SCALES

The primary major scale is the C major scale (C, D, E, F, G, A, B, C). It is constructed from the primary tone row. Modeled after it, all major scales follow the same established pattern of whole and half steps. A major scale can be created from any note.

- **The major scales with sharps** are the scales that use sharps to alter—raise the tones to preserve the major scale's whole/half step pattern. Each subsequent scale is created from the **upper P5** (the 5th degree) of the previous scale.
- **The major scales with flats** are the scales that use flats to alter—lower the tones to preserve the major scale's whole/half step pattern. Each subsequent scale is created from the **lower P5** or its inversion the upper P4 (the 4th degree) of the previous scale.

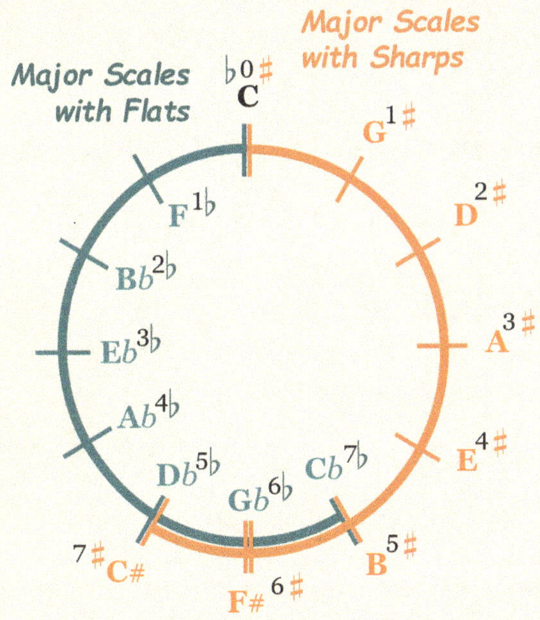

E   Write the names of the major scales with sharps and flats.

Major Scales with Sharps: ____

Major Scales with Flats: ____

MAJOR SCALES

C major is the **primary major scale**. It consists of the tones of the **primary tone row**. Besides C major, we have **seven major scales with sharps** and **seven with flats**.

All major scales are composed of **two parts** known as **tetrachords**. Each tetrachord follows a specific pattern of whole and half steps. **Major scales** consist of two **identical tetrachords** featuring a 1-1-1/2 pattern. The tetrachords are **separated** by a **whole step**.

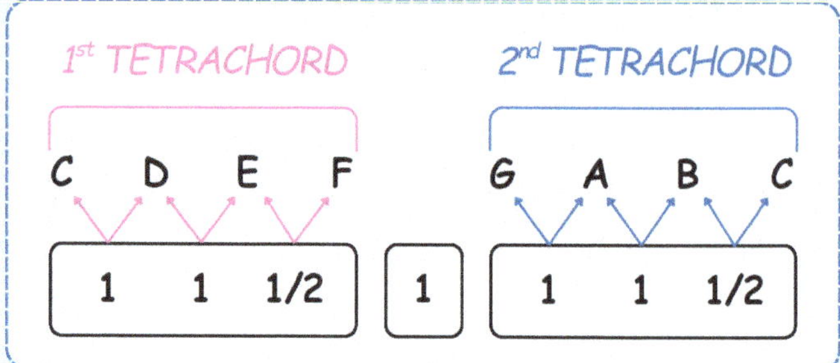

The neighboring major scales always **share one tetrachord**. Major scales with **sharps** progressing in ascending motion share their **second (upper) tetrachord** with the subsequent scale, while major scales with **flats** progressing downwards share their **first (lower) tetrachord** with the subsequent scale.

Major Scales with Sharps – *The Second Tetrachord Becomes the First (Lower) of the Next Scale*

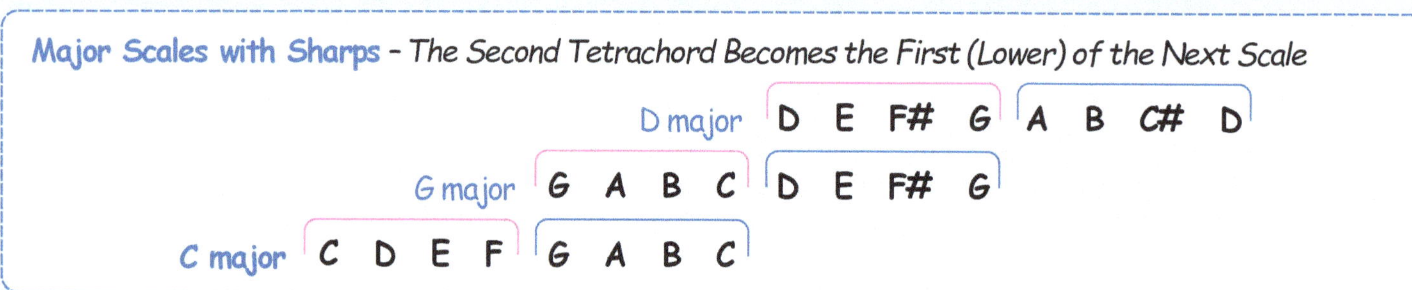

Major Scales with Flats – *The First Tetrachord Becomes the Second (Upper) of the Next Scale*

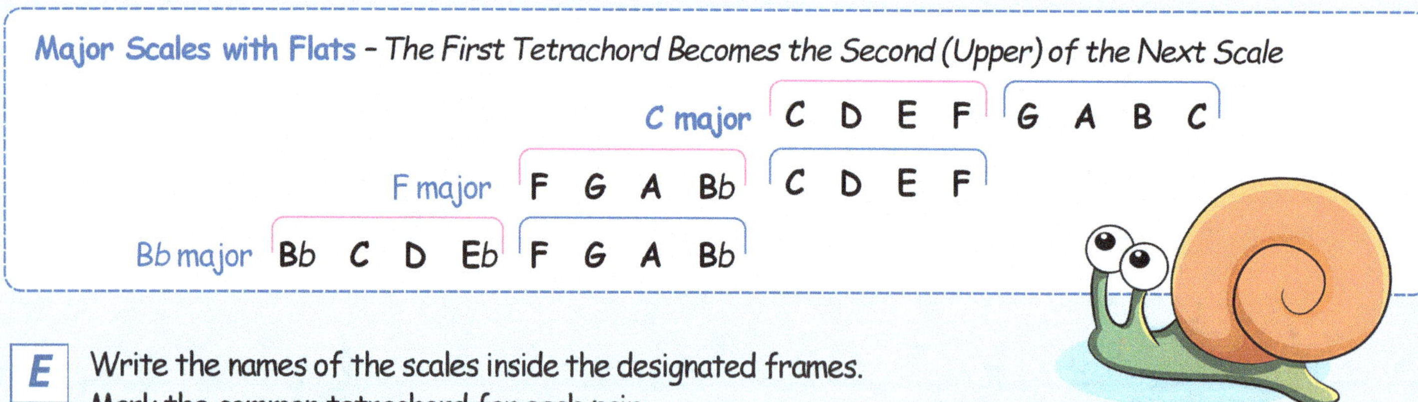

E Write the names of the scales inside the designated frames. Mark the common tetrachord for each pair.

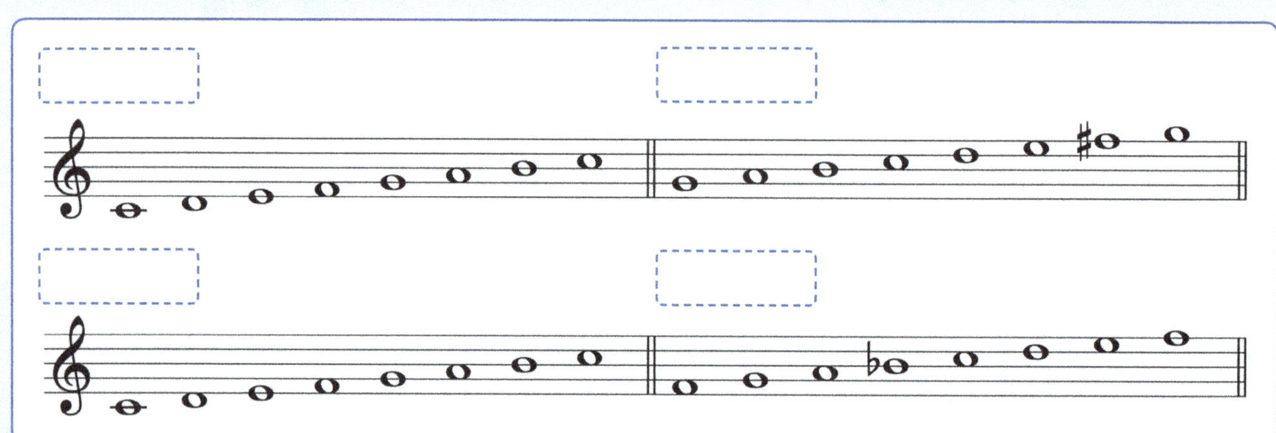

SCALES WITH 5, 6, AND 7 FLATS

The major scales with flats are those with notes altered down using flats. In the previous Notebook we have learned the scales up to four flats: **F major** (1b), **B flat major** (2b), **E flat major** (3b), and **A flat major** (4b). The remaining major scales with flats are: **D flat major** (5b), **G flat major** (6b), and **C flat major** (7b).

D♭ major
- key signature - **5 flats** - **Bb, Eb, Ab, Db,** and **Gb**
- The major scales with flats: F, Bb, Eb, Ab, **Db**, Gb, Cb.

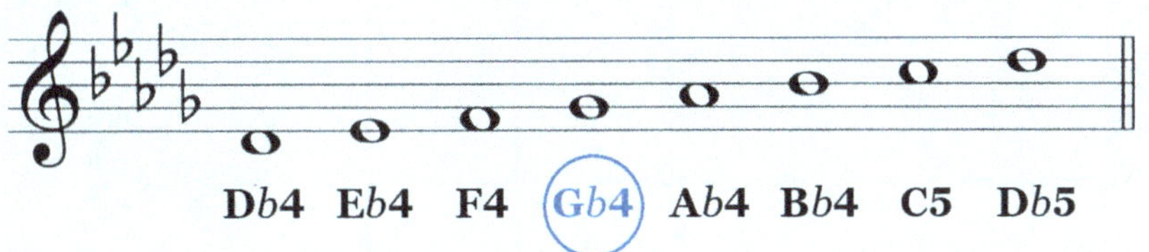

The new flat is always added to the fourth step (degree).

G♭ major
- key signature - **6 flats** - **Bb, Eb, Ab, Db, Gb,** and **Cb**
- The major scales with flats: F, Bb, Eb, Ab, Db, **Gb**, Cb.

C♭ major
- key signature - **7 flats** - **Bb, Eb, Ab, Db, Gb, Cb,** and **Fb**
- The major scales with flats: I, Bb, Eb, Ab, Db, Gb, **Cb**.

E   Notate the tonic fifth chords and their inversions.

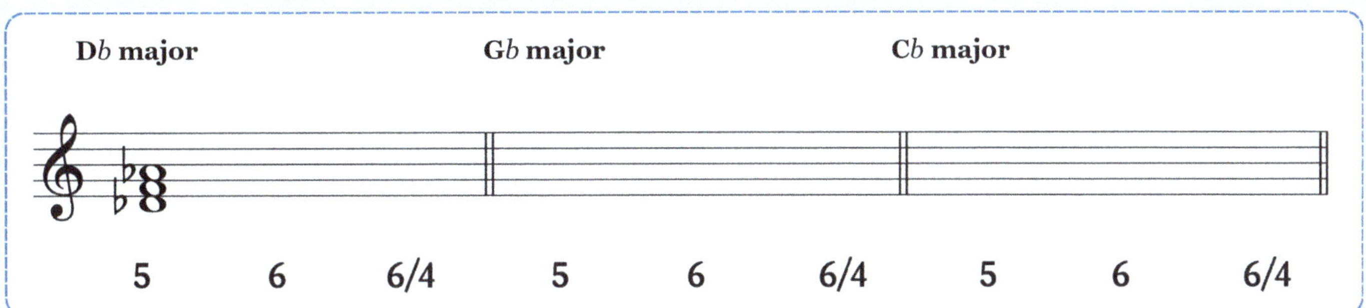

EXCERCISES

E Fill in the table with all the major scales with flats, following the provided example.

scale name	number of flats	tonic fifth chord		
C major	0	C	E	G
F major	1			

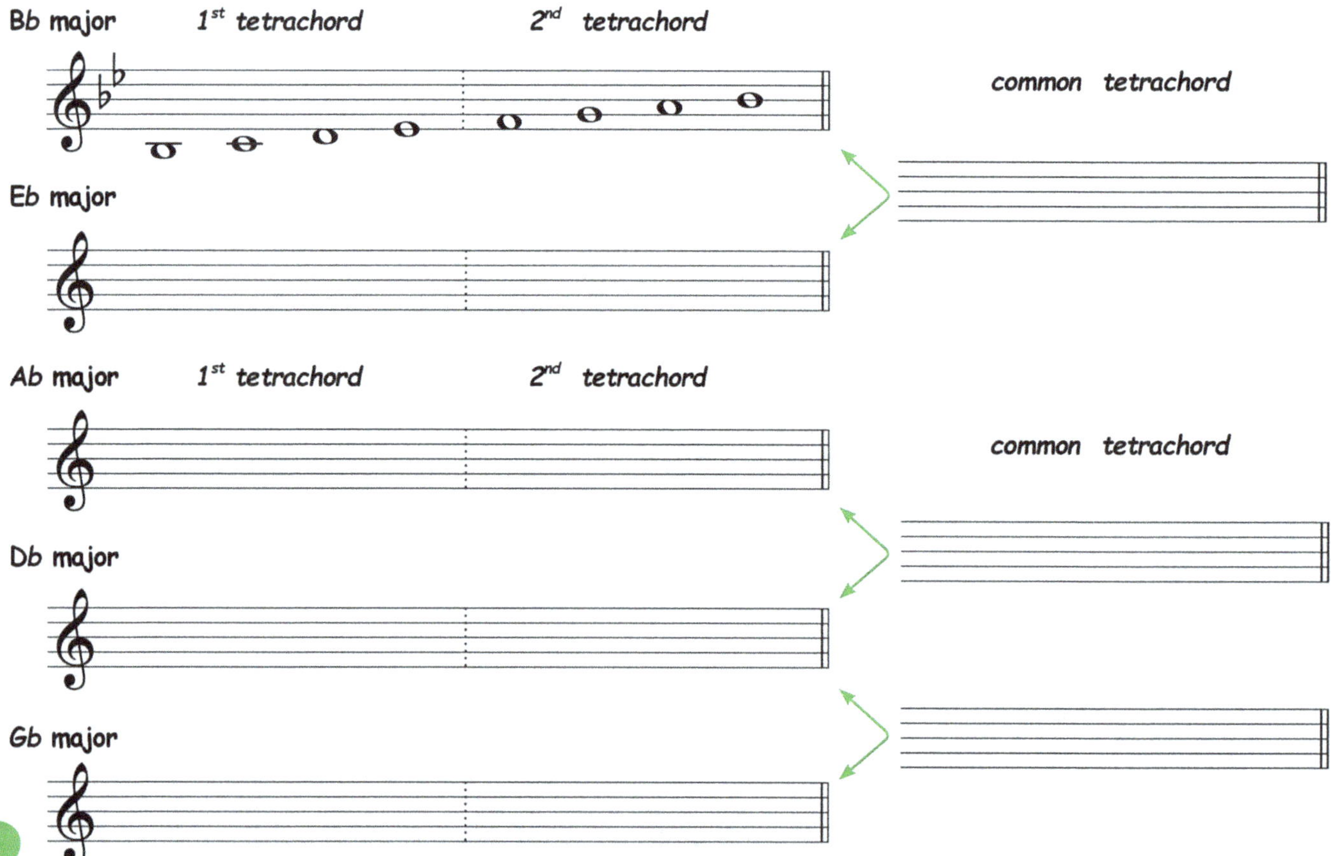

E Notate the subsequent scales. Identify and notate their common tetrachords.

Play For Me, Fiddler Boy

E Learn the song "Play for me, Fiddler Boy." Practice clapping, singing, and playing triplets (*Clefi's Music Notebook 2*). Identify and fill in the names of the keys into which the opening section of the song has been transposed.

E The major fifth chord and its inversions.
Write the numeric symbols identifying the inversions under each chord (5, 6, 6/4).

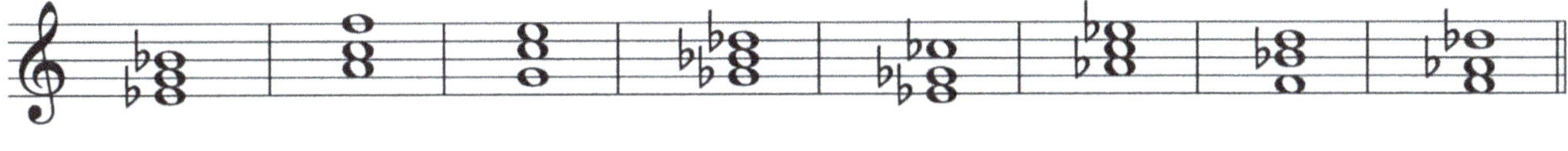

E Review the harmonic functions (*Clefi's Music Notebook 2*).
What are the names of the three fundamental scale degrees (T, S, D)?

Notate fifth chords from the fundamental degrees according to the assignment.

F major   Eb major   Db major

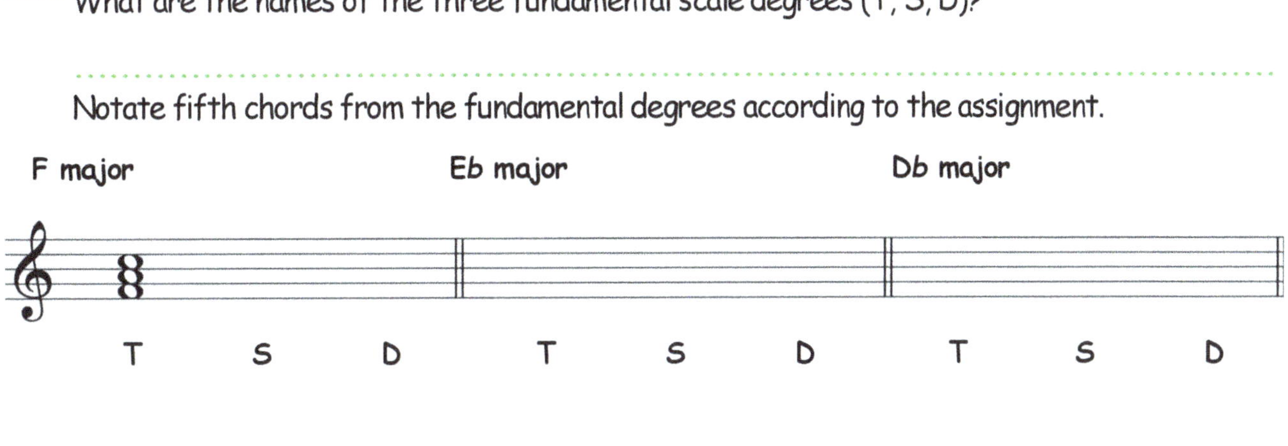

NOTATION

Notation refers to the recording off a musical composition through the use of **music notation** (musical symbols). **Notes** and **rests** are placed on a **musical staff**. At the beginning of the staff, we must place a **music clef**, which establishes the pitch and the register for reading the notes.

Most instrumentalists and vocalists (singgers) primarily read music in treble and bass clefs. The notation for each instrument is based on its **range**, which is defined by the **lowest and highest notes** that the instrument can produce. The same principle applies to the singing voices.

SINGING VOICES - vocals

Singing voices are categorized into four distinct groups based on their vocal range:

S	**soprano**	high female voice
A	**alto**	low female voice
T	**tenor**	higher male voice
B	**bass**	low male voice

Children's voices are divided into two groups only: **higher - soprano**, and **lower - alto**. Vocal parts are notated primarily in treble and bass clefs.

Overview of the Basic Notes in Bass and Treble Clefs

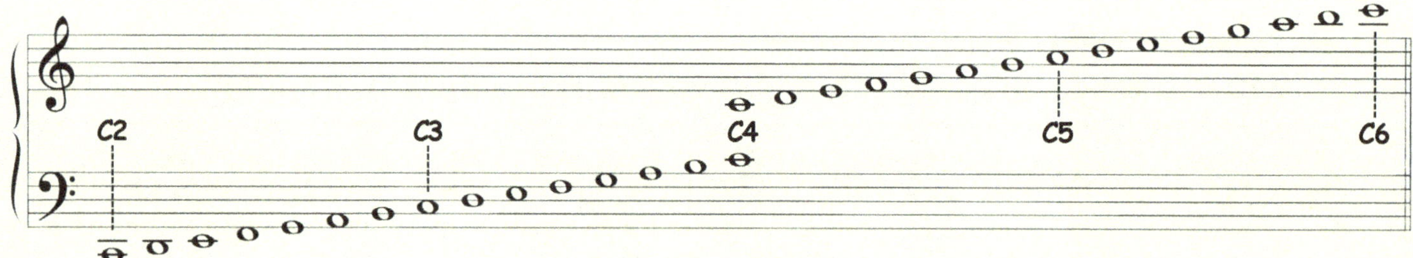

E Notate the notes in the treble and bass clefs according to the assignments.

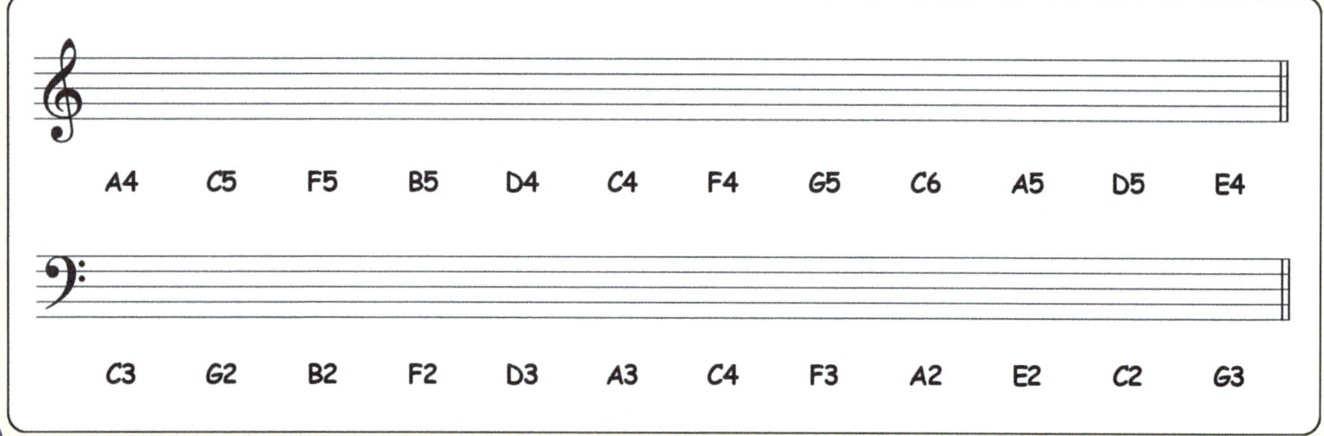

NOTATION FOR VARIOUS MUSICAL INSTRUMENTS

Piano notation uses two clefs:

G clef - treble clef   Used for the upper (right) part of the keyboard and usually played by the right hand.

F clef - bass clef   Used for the lower (left) part of the keyboard and usually played by the left hand.

Musicians read the notes based on the clef that indicates their notated pitches. Pianists, organists, harpsichordists, and other keyboard players must be able to read both clefs simultaneously.

Most instruments typically have their scores and parts notated on a single staff, utilizing the clef that corresponds to their specific range. However, instruments with a wider range often use multiple clefs. For instance, cellists need to be proficient in reading three clefs: **bass, tenor,** and **treble.**

High-pitch instruments (violin, flute, etc.) use the **treble clef.**
Low-pitch instruments (double bass, tuba, etc.) use **the bass clef**.

Alto and **tenor** (mid-range) **instruments**, such as the viola or cello, also use C clefs - the alto and tenor clefs. The C clef is the last remaining movable clef, and it's essential to note its placement on the staff. The small arrow connecting the two Cs indicates the position of the C4 note.

Alto C clef - the arrow points to the middle line
Tenor C clef - the arrow points to the fourth line

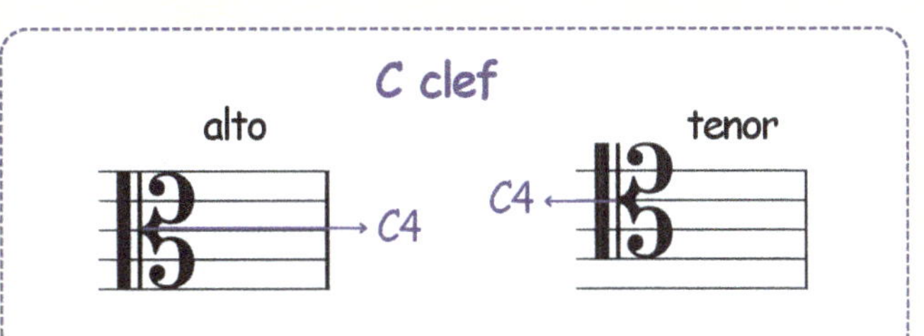

Drawing the C clef:

The illustration of how the C4 note is notated in all standard clefs.

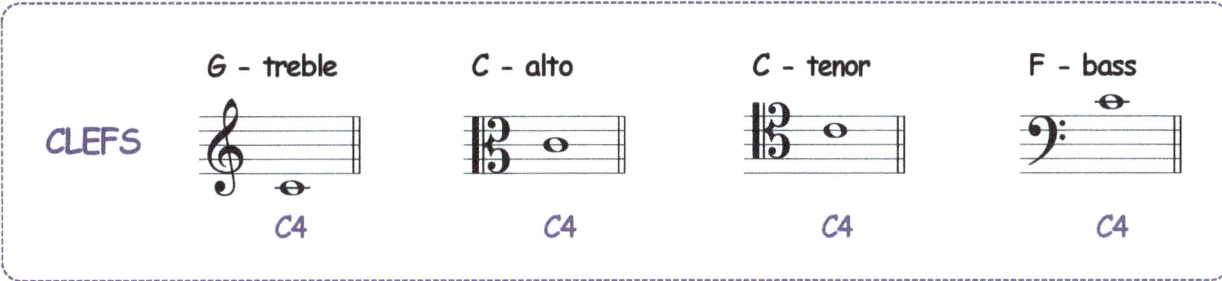

PRIMARY & ALTERED TONES

The **Primary Tones** are the tones of the musical alphabet - *C, D, E, F, G, A, B.*

The **Altered Tones** are the raised or lowered primary tones. Each primary tone can be raise or lowered by one half or two half steps *(a whole step)* using accidentals.

Accidentals include **single** and **double sharps** and **flats** and **naturals**. An accidental is placed before the note we need to alter and is valid for the **duration of a measure**. The validity of an accidental can be erased by placing a natural or a different accidental before an altered note.

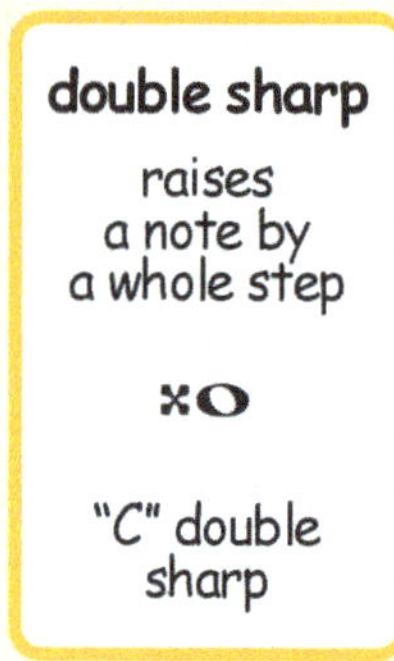

Utilizing Accidentals Within a Measure

Using accidentals within a measure can be tricky. It's essential to consider the **key signature** and any **previous accidentals** used within that measure. While modern notation software and applications handle much of the work for us, understanding how to apply accidentals correctly is crucial for **accurate and clear notation**.

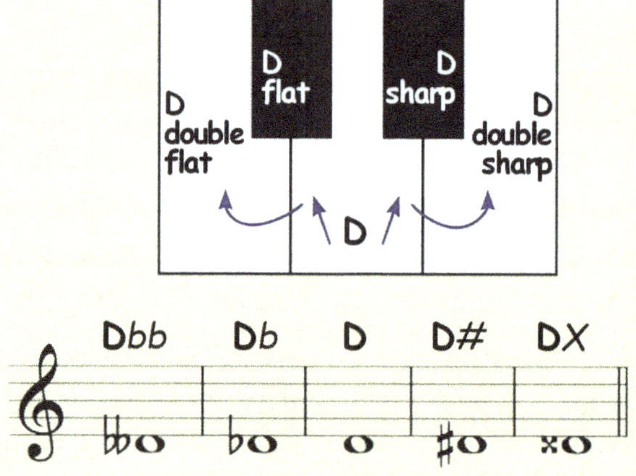

Example:

E Write the correct name of the notes on the dotted lines below the staff.

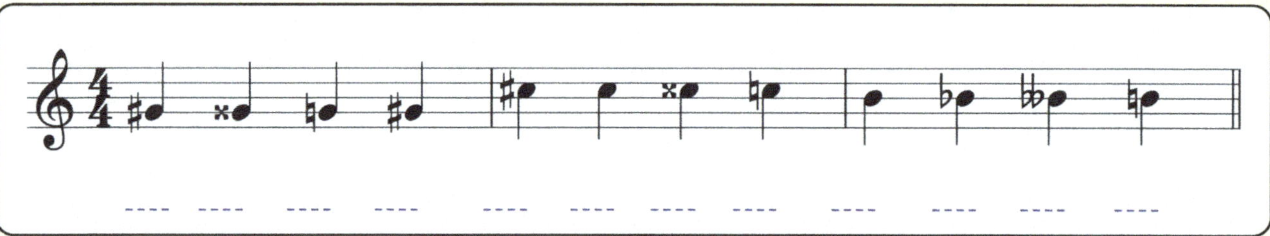

WRITING NOTES & ACCIDENTALS

Accidentals are placed in front of the note to which they belong.
Accidentals must be placed in exactly the same place as their note.

E Practice: accidentals on the line   accidentals in the space

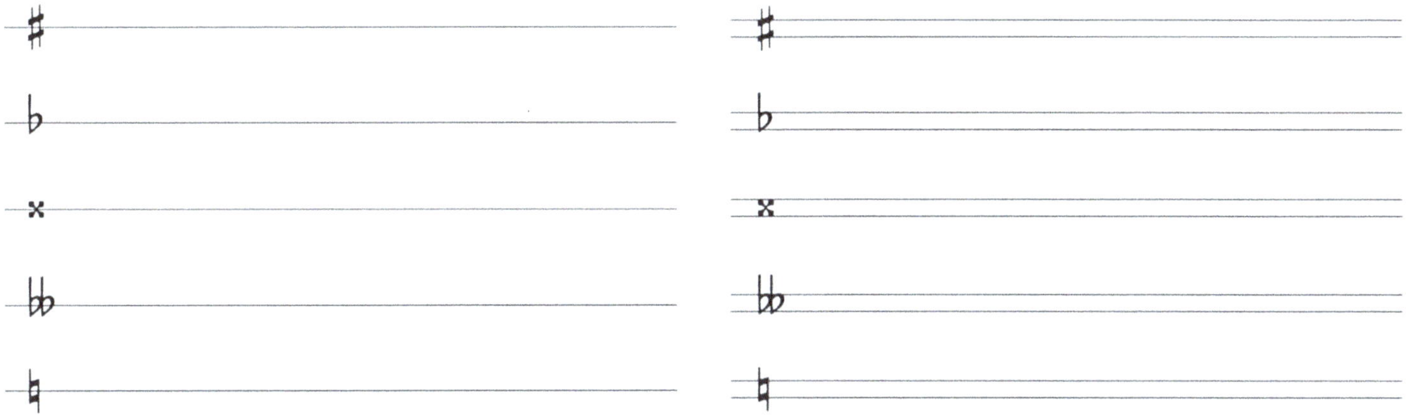

E Notate quarter notes according to the assignments.
Pay attention to the use of accidentals within a measure!

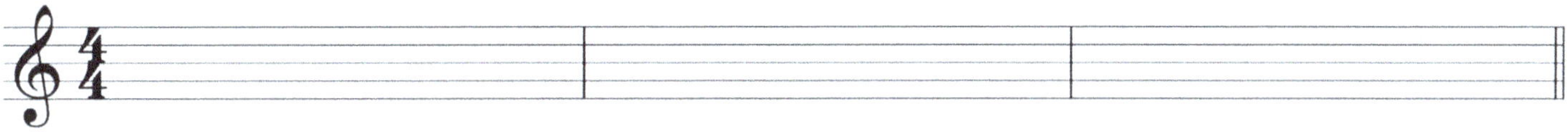

F#4   F4   G#4   GX4   G#4   G#4   G4   DX4   Eb4   Ebb4   Eb4   E4

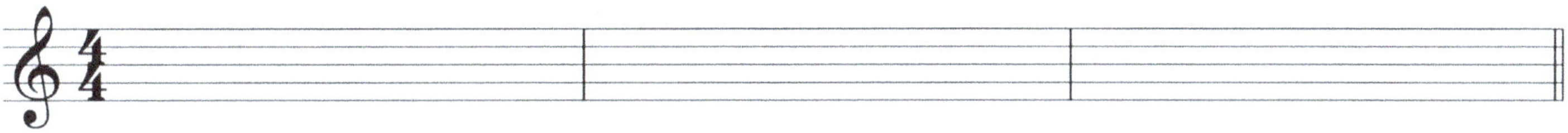

Db5   Bb4   Bbb4   B4   D5   D#5   D#5   DX5   Gb4   Ab4   Abb4   G4

E Fill in the measure lines, then circle in red all wrongly notated notes in both clefs.

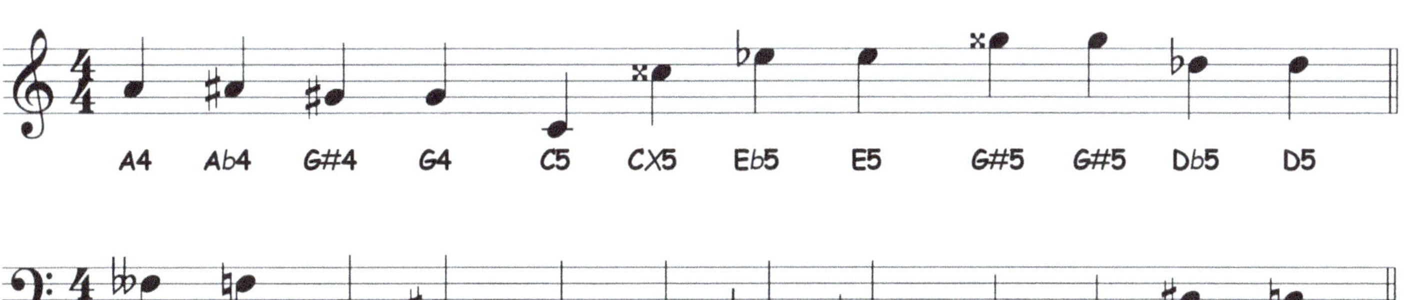

A4   Ab4   G#4   G4   C5   CX5   Eb5   E5   G#5   G#5   Db5   D5

Fb3   F3   C3   CX3   B2   Bb2   Bbb2   B2   G2   G#2   D#3   D#3

DERIVED INTERVALS

Intervals can be **primary** and **derived**. When determining intervals, we use the tones of the major scale, for example, the C major scale - C, D, E, F, G, A, B, C. The primary intervals are those between the tonic and all other tones of the major scale. These intervals are divided into perfect and major.

Derived intervals are **altered primary intervals**. They can be either **bigger** or **smaller**, and they can be created by raising or lowering one of the tones of the primary intervals.

PERFECT INTERVALS AND THE INTERVALS DERIVED FROM THEM

The **perfect intervals** are the **unison**, **fourth**, **fifth**, and **octave**. The perfect intervals belong to the primary intervals. The intervals derived from the perfect intervals are the augmented (bigger) and diminished (smaller) intervals.

- **Augmented intervals** are a half step larger than their perfect primary interval.
  Their symbol is either "+," "**a**," or "**aug**."
- **Diminished intervals** are a half step smaller than their perfect primary interval.
  Their symbol is either "°," "**d**", or "**dim**."

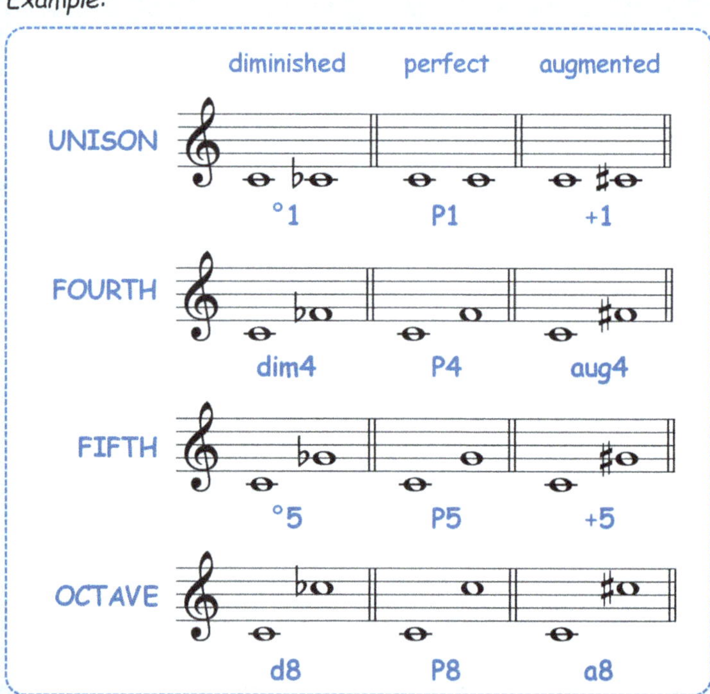

The primary and their derived intervals must have the same note in their naming.
For example, a perfect 4th is C-F, an augmented 4th is C-F# (not Gb), and a diminished 4th is C-Fb (not E).

E Create perfect intervals and their derived augmented and diminished versions as assigned.

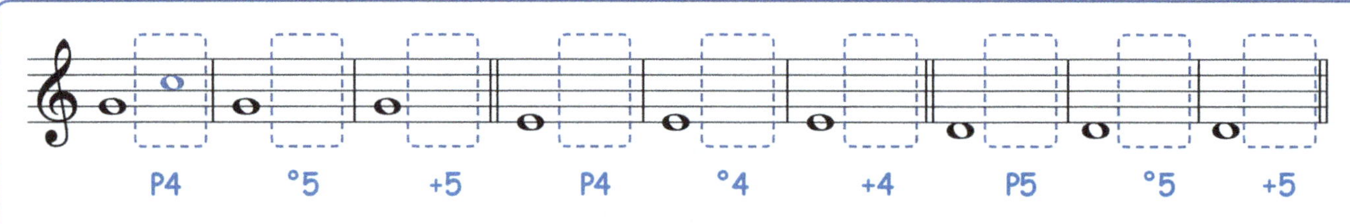

MAJOR INTERVALS AND THE INTERVALS DERIVED FROM THEM

The **major intervals** include the **second**, **third**, **sixth**, and **seventh**. They are part of the primary intervals.
Major intervals can be lowered by a half step to become **minor intervals**.
The **minor intervals** are derived intervals; however, they are just as important as the primary major intervals.

The major and minor intervals can be further derived into the augmented (bigger than major) and diminished (smaller than minor) intervals.

- **Augmented intervals** are a half step larger than their major primary interval.
  Their symbol is either "+," "**a**", or "**aug**."
- **Diminished intervals** are a half step smaller than their minor primary interval.
  Their symbol is either "**d**" or "**dim**."

Example:

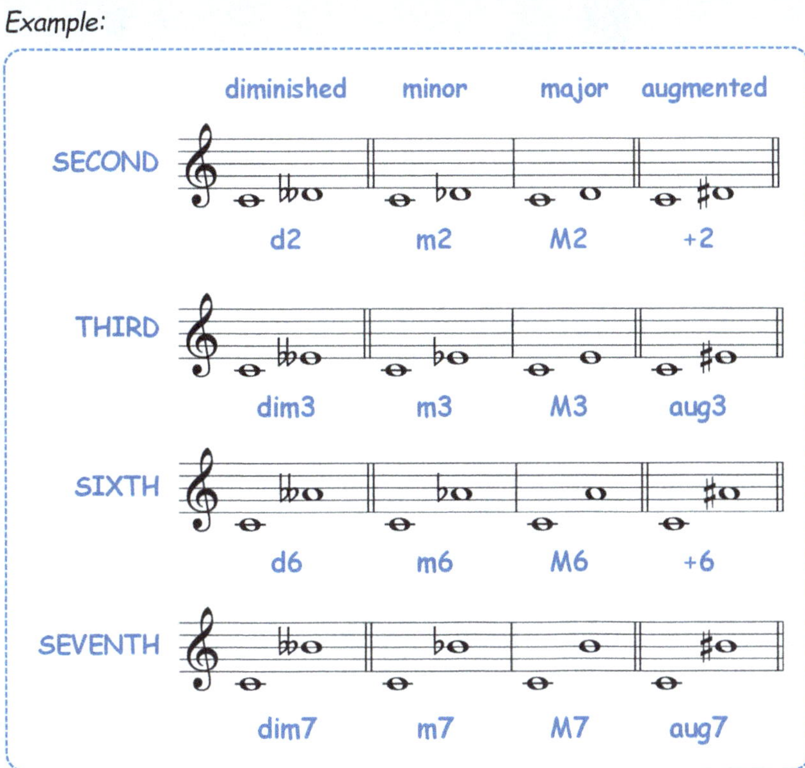

E   Create the assigned intervals from the note G4.

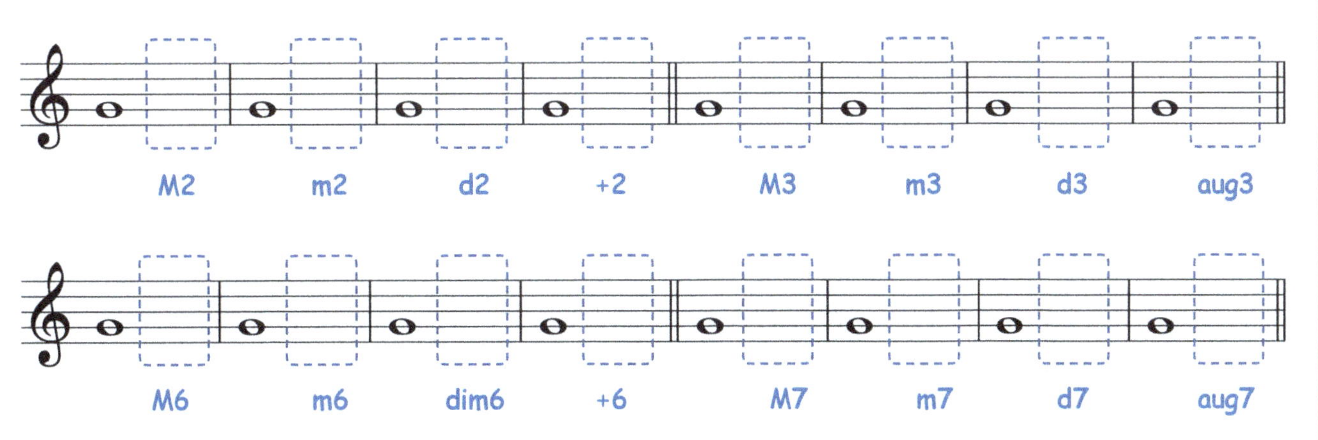

ENHARMONIC EXCHANGE

ENHARMONIC TONES

Enharmonic (pitch equivalent) tones are tones that sound exactly the same but have different names. We describe them as **enharmonically exchangeable** because they can be used interchangeably.

Example:

*When we play tones **C#** and **Db**, we play the same key, however, the music notation will look like this:*

C#4 Db4

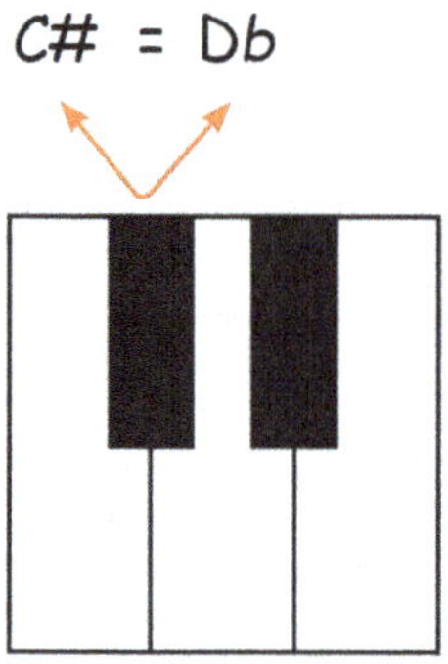

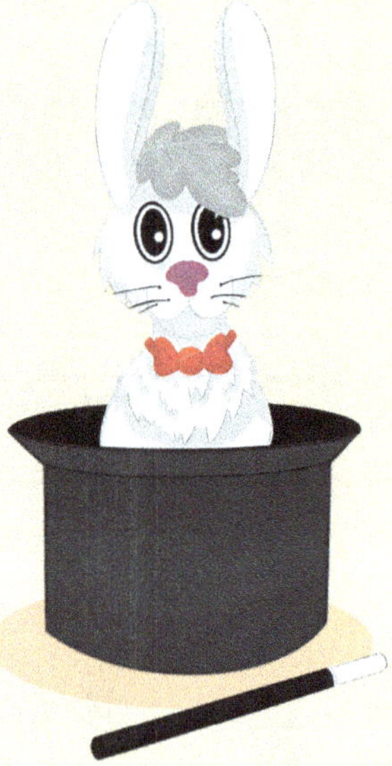

The tones **C sharp** and **D flat** are interchangeable, as they are **enharmonically equivalent**. Here are some additional examples of enharmonic tones:

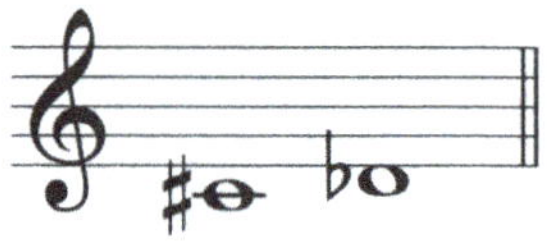

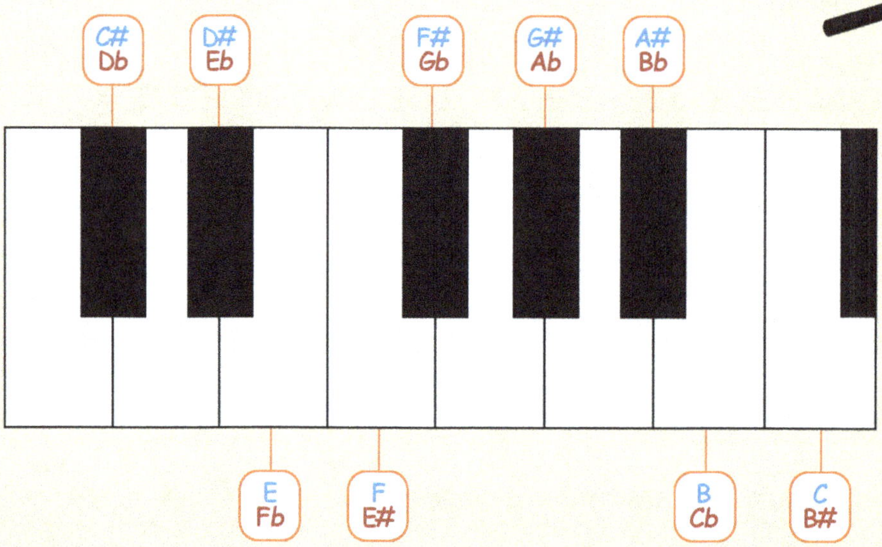

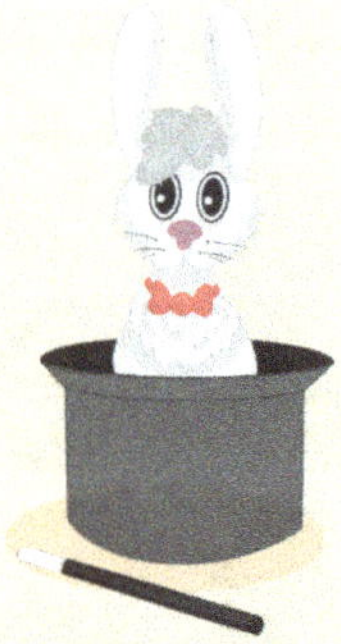

E Write the enharmonically equivalent notes that correspond to the notes on the staffs.

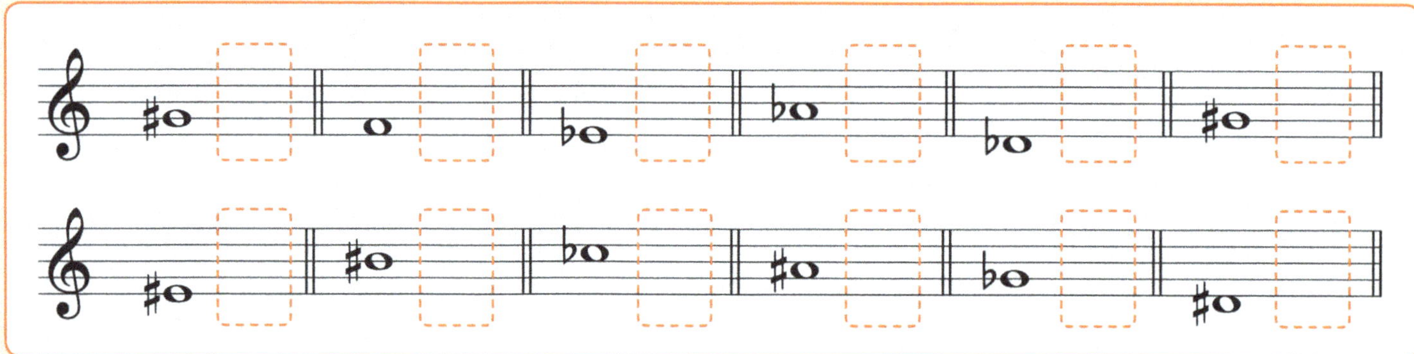

ENHARMONIC SCALES

Enharmonic scales are scales that sound exactly the same but are differently notated. We also call them enharmonically exchangeable scales because they can be freely interchanged.

The enharmonically exchangeable scales have enharmonically **interchangeable foundational tones - tonics**, which means that they have **different names**.

Enharmonically interchangeable scale:

B major	=	C flat major
F sharp major	=	G flat major
C sharp major	=	D flat major

C major	
1# G major	F major 1b
2# D major	B major 2b
3# A major	Eb major 3b
4# E major	Ab major 4b
5# B major	Db major 5b
6# F# major	Gb major 6b
7# C# major	Cb major 7b

We have a total of **15 major scales**: *C* major and **seven major scales with sharps** and **seven with flats**. However, in practice, there are only **12 distinct major scales**, as three of the sharp scales are **enharmonically interchangeable** with three flat scales. These paired scales sound exactly the same.

Fascinating Fact for Math Enthusiasts

B major	5#	F# major	6#	C# major	7#
Cb major	7b	Gb major	6b	Db major	5b
	12		12		12

The number 12 is a magical figure in music theory. Here, it pops up as the total number of accidentals between the scales paired as enharmonically (pitch equivalent) interchangeable.

Clefi & Notelina's Songbook, pg. 61

E Notate the melody in assigned keys, then listen and compare them.

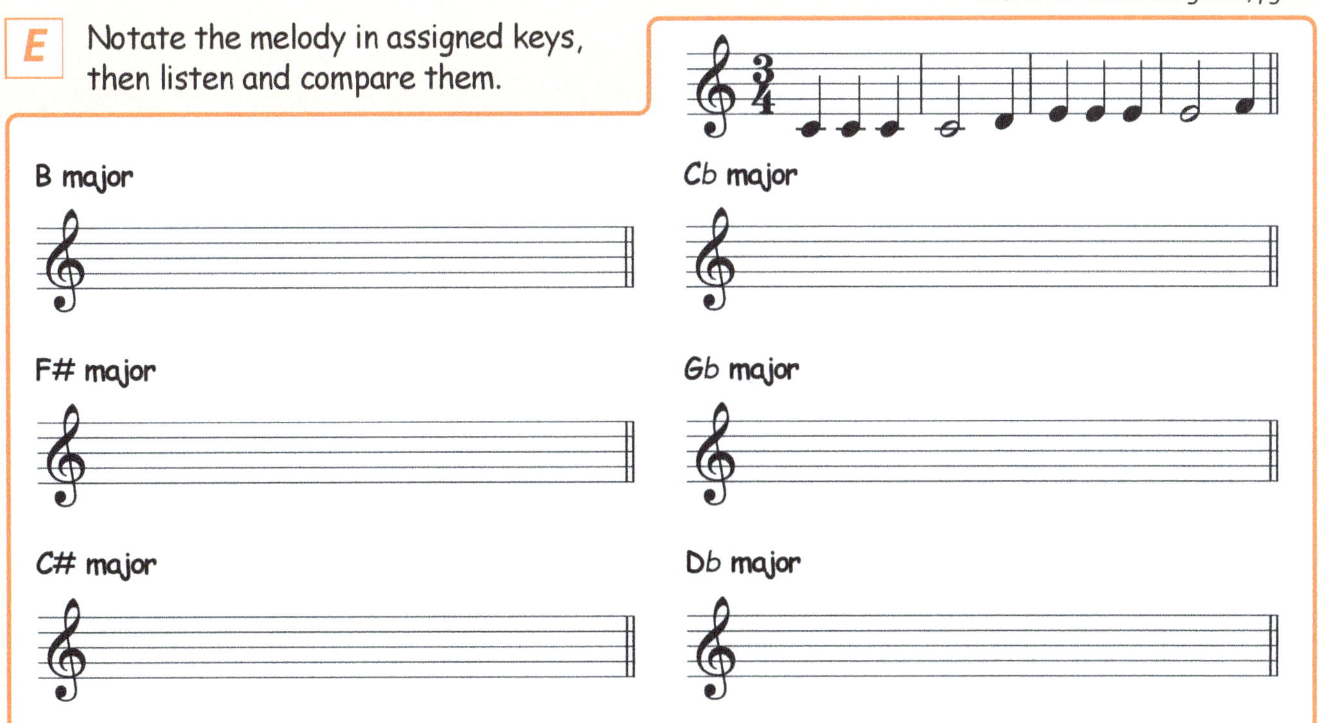

EXCERCISES

So Very Deep and Wide

NOTATION

E Learn the song "So Very Deep and Wide." Identify the notes in both clefs.

PRIMMARY AND DERIVED TONES

E Circle all wrongly identified notes in red.

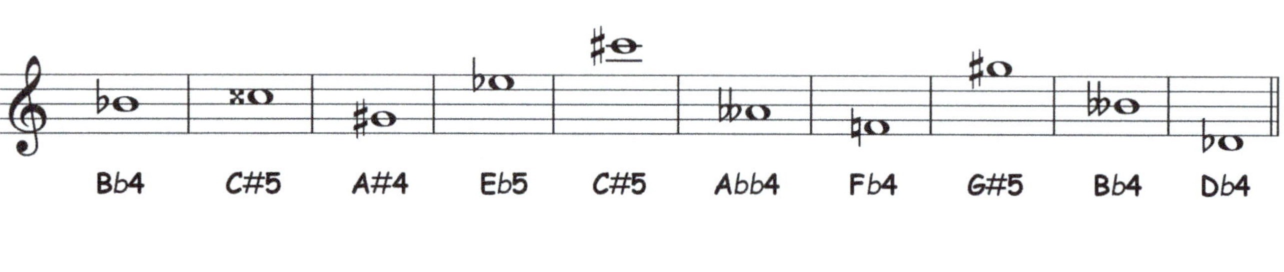

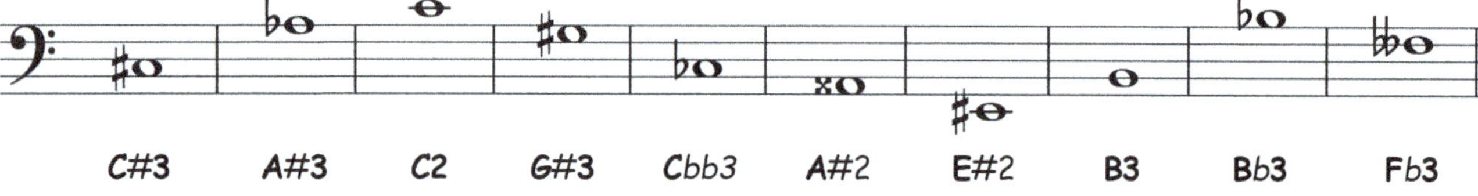

PRIMARY AND DERIVED INTERVALS

E Identify and label the intervals. Color the boxes with the primary intervals red and the boxes with the derived intervals yellow.

Perfect Intervals and Derived Intervals from Them

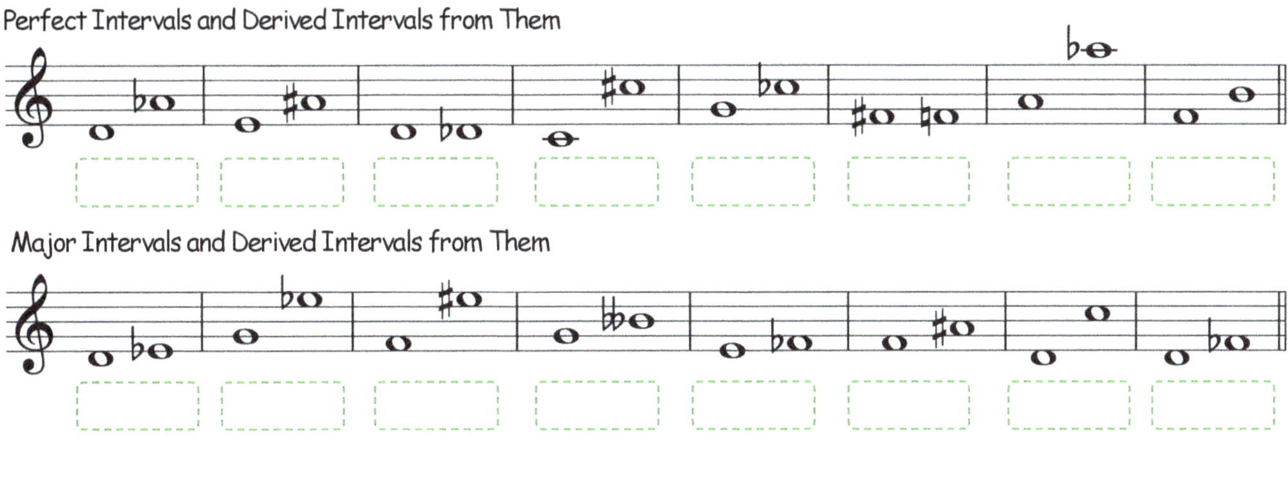

Major Intervals and Derived Intervals from Them

ENHARMONIC EXCHANGE

E Connect the corresponding enharmonic tones.

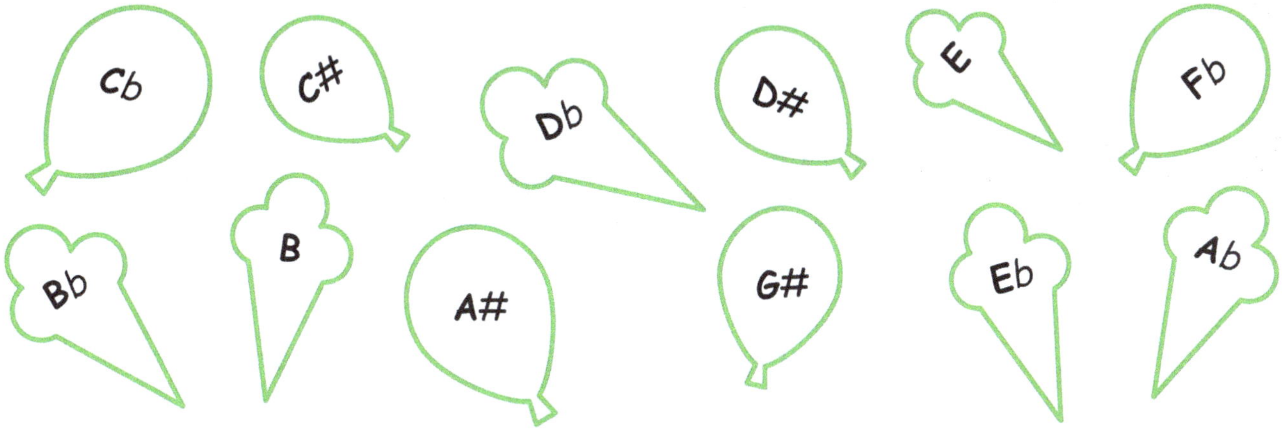

E Write the names of the keys into the boxes next to the opening section of the song "So Very Deep and Wide." Connect the boxes with enharmonically interchangeable keys.

Clefi & Notelina's Songbook, pg. 83

MAJOR & MINOR SCALES

Major and minor scales are the most commonly used scales in Western music.

Major scales have a major mode (sounding open and happy). Their fundamental interval is M3.

The major scales' music symbol is the uppercase letter marking the T (tonic) degree (**C** = C major).

Minor scales have a minor mode (sounding melancholy and sad). Their fundamental interval is m3.

The minor scales' music symbol is the uppercase letter marking T followed by a lowercase "m" (**Cm** = C minor.

Major and minor scales share some common traits.

- **Relative scales** = same key signature
- **Parallel scales** = same letter in their names (same tonic tone).

RELATIVE SCALES

Every major scale has its relative minor scale.

Relative scales share these common traits:

- same tones
- same key signature
- one is major the other is natural minor
- the minor scale's tonic is the 6th degree of its relative major scale

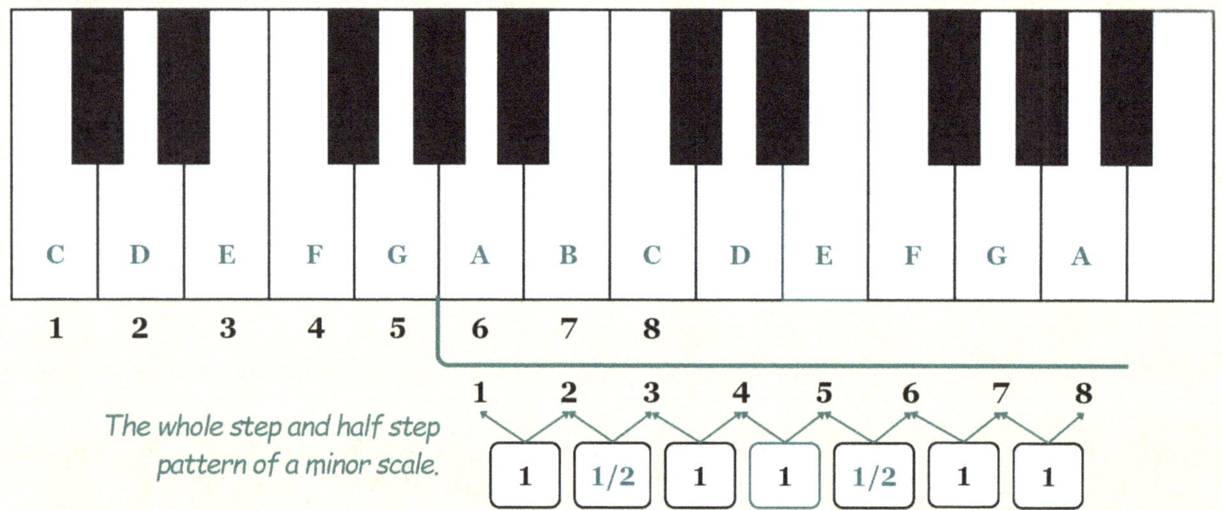

The whole step and half step pattern of a minor scale.

*The **relative scale** created simply by moving the tonic of a major scale is called the **natural minor** scale or by its ancient Greek name **Aeolian**.*

E Notate the primary major and minor scales (see the keyboard). Bracket the half steps.

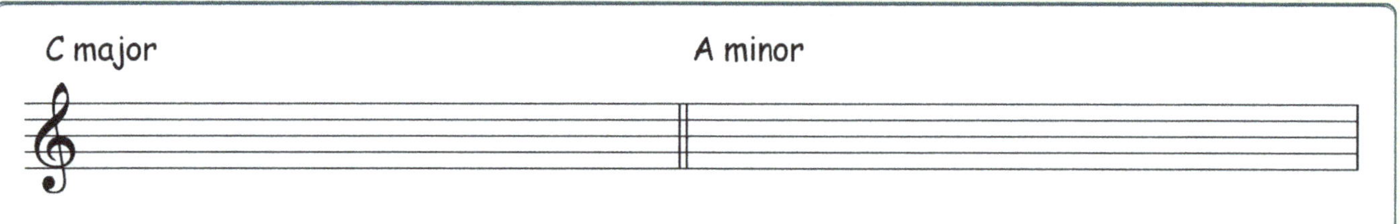

MAJOR & MINOR FIFTH CHORD

A **fifth chord** is a triad that contains a third and a fifth,
with a perfect fifth between its bottom and top notes.
The **tonic fifth chord** is built on the first degree of any scale,
whether major or minor, and is considered the foundational chord.

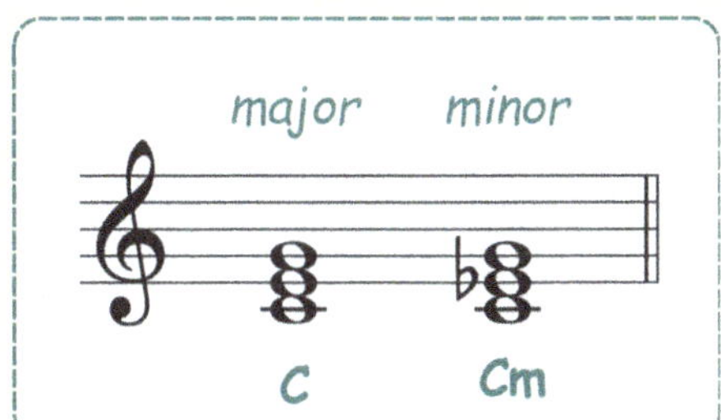

MAJOR AND MINOR FIFTH CHORD

Both major and minor fifth chords contain a perfect fifth between
the outer tones of the chord; however, the thirds are different.
- A **major fifth chord** contains a **major third** and a **perfect fifth**.
  Its chord symbol is the uppercase letter - **C** for C major.
- A **minor fifth chord** contains minor third and perfect fifth.
  Its chord symbol is uppercase letter followed by the lowercase "m" - **Cm** for C minor.

FIFTH CHORD INVERSIONS

Fifth chord **inversions** are formed by raising the lowest note by an octave.
- Root position: a **fifth chord** - **5**
- First inversion: a **sixth chord** - **6**
- Second inversion: a **four–sixth chord** - **6/4**

Examples built from the note C:

a **major** fifth chord and its inversions

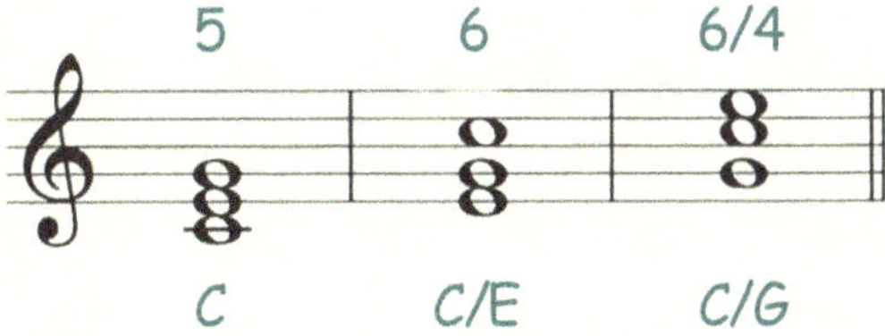

a **minor** fifth chord and its inversions

The chord symbol for inversions consists of two attributes separated by a forward slash:
the chord symbol of the root tone / the bass note

E Practice recognizing both major and minor fifth chords. Circle all minor fifth chords in green.

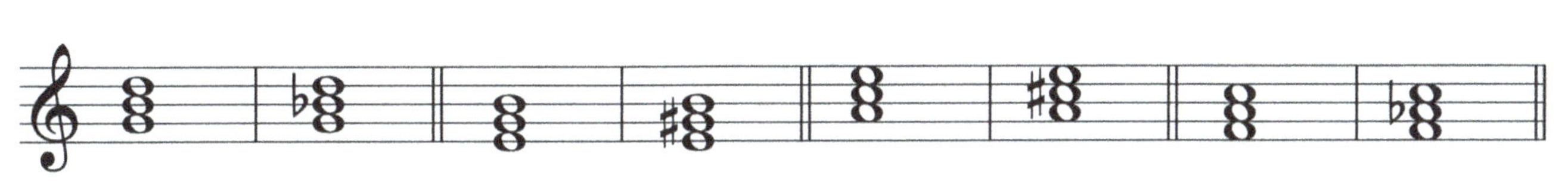

PRIMARY MINOR SCALE

The primary minor scale is the **A minor scale**. The A minor scale is the **relative minor** to the C major scale. Both of these scales contain the **tones of the primary tone row**. They have no key signature.

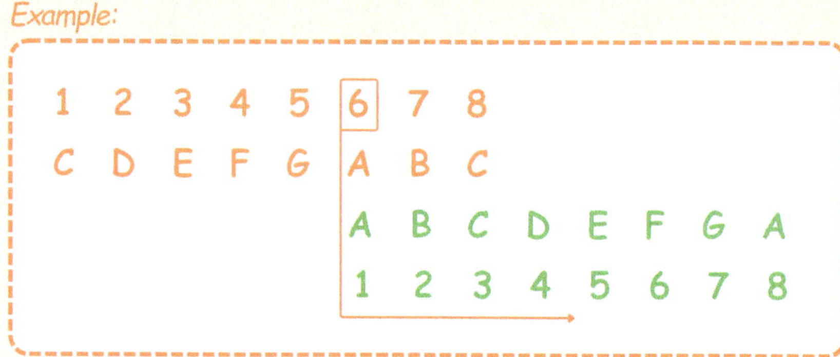

*When we spell out or play the tones of a major scale starting from its **sixth degree**,*
*we get the **natural minor scale**.*
*Natural minor scales have the **same notes** as their relative major scales.*

The Tetrachords of a Natural Minor Scale

A natural minor scale has half steps between the **2nd** and **3rd** and the **5th** and **6th** degrees.

We can build a minor scale from **any tone**. As with the major scales, it is important to observe the **whole-step-half-step pattern**. To preserve the pattern and the structure of **minor scale tetrachords**, some notes must be raised or lowered.

Just like major scales, minor scales are those with sharps and those with flats. The sharp minor scales use sharps to alter their notes. The flat minor scales use flats.

In addtion to the primary minor scale (A minor), there are **seven minor scales with sharps** and **seven with flats**.
The sharps and flats are added to the subsequent minor scales in the **same order** as with the major scales.

A minor scale has **three distinct forms**:
- **Natural Minor Scale**: This scale has no alterations.
- **Harmonic Minor Scale**: Features a **raised 7th degree**, both ascending and descending.
- **Melodic Minor Scale**: Includes raised **6th** and **7th degrees** when **ascending**, and follows the **natural scale** when **descending**.

The **original minor scale** is known as the **natural minor scale**, which is also referred to by its ancient Greek name, the **Aeolian scale**. To incorporate the harmonic traits of a major scale, the natural minor scale underwent a notable evolution. To meet both harmonic and melodic requirements, two **derived minor scales** emerged: the **harmonic minor scale** and the **melodic minor scale**.

Derived Harmonic and Melodic Minor Scales

- Both scales share the **same key signature** as the natural minor.
- The **first tetrachord is the same for all three scales** (a half step between the 2nd and 3rd degrees).
- Each minor scale has a **unique second tetrachord**.
- Note alterations should always be made using **free-standing accidentals**, including the reversion of the melodic minor scale 6th and 7th degrees to their natural scale positions while descending.

E — In all three scale, mark all raised (altered) notes in red.
For the descending melodic scale, circle the notes with naturals canceling the sharps in green.

A natural minor (Aeolian)

A harmonic minor (rasied 7th degree)

A melodic minor (raised 6th and 7th degrees on the way up, lowered on the way down (the natural minor form)

The harmonic minor scale is the only scale with the 1½ step distance (the augmented second) between two notes. It's an uncommon skip for a scale easily recognizable by ear.

E — Fill in the name of the harmonic scale to the designated spaces on the keyboard. Mark the tones separated by the interval of augmented second (1½ step) with a red bracket.

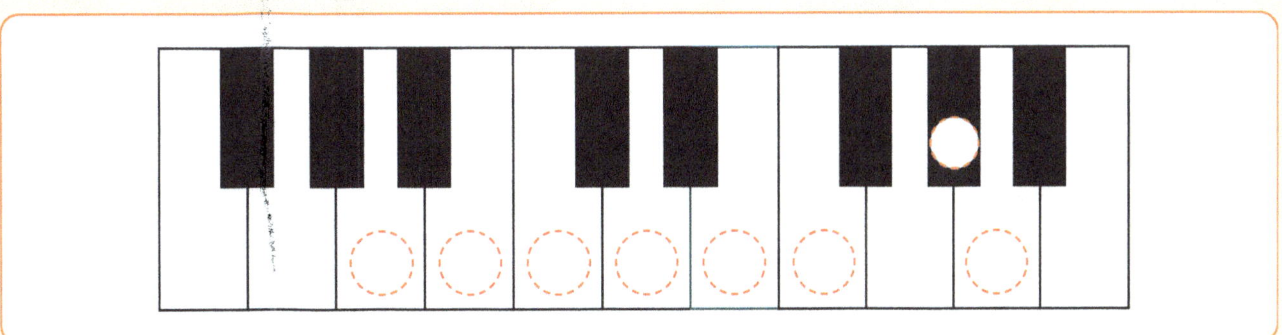

Minor Scales with Sharps

The minor scales with sharps originate from the A minor scale, building upon the P5 (the fifth degree) of the preceding scale. Every subsequent scale has one more sharp. The sharps are added in the following order: F#, C#, G#, A#, E#, B#.

Minor scales with sharps are:

E, B, F sharp, C sharp, G sharp, D sharp, and A sharp minor.

MAJOR & MINOR SCALES

Relative Scales

Relative major and minor scales have the **same key signature**.
Relative scales have the **same position** on the Circle of Fifths.

Parallel Scales

Parallel major and minor scales have the **same name** but a **different key signature**.
To determine the key signature using the relationship between two parallel scales, we have to jump three degrees anti-clockwise on the Circle of Fifths.

Example: E major = 4# (4-3=1) - E minor = 1#
F major = 1b (1+3=4) - F minor = 4b

On the Circle of Fifths, you'll notice that sharps diminish while flats increase as you move in a counterclockwise direction. Be sure to explore this on both pages!

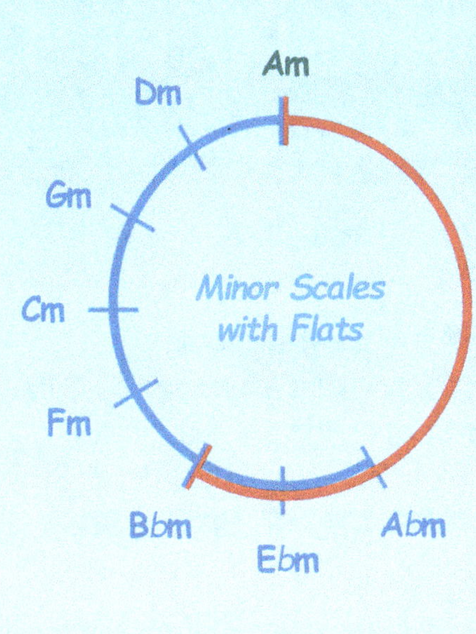

Minor Scales with Flats

The minor scales with flats originate from the A minor scale, building upon the lower P5 or its inversion the upper P4 (the fourth degree) of the preceding scale. Every subsequent scale has one more flat. The flats are added in the following order: Bb, Eb, Ab, Db, Gb, Cb, Fb.

Minor scales with flats are:
D, G, C, F, B flat, E flat, and A flat minor.

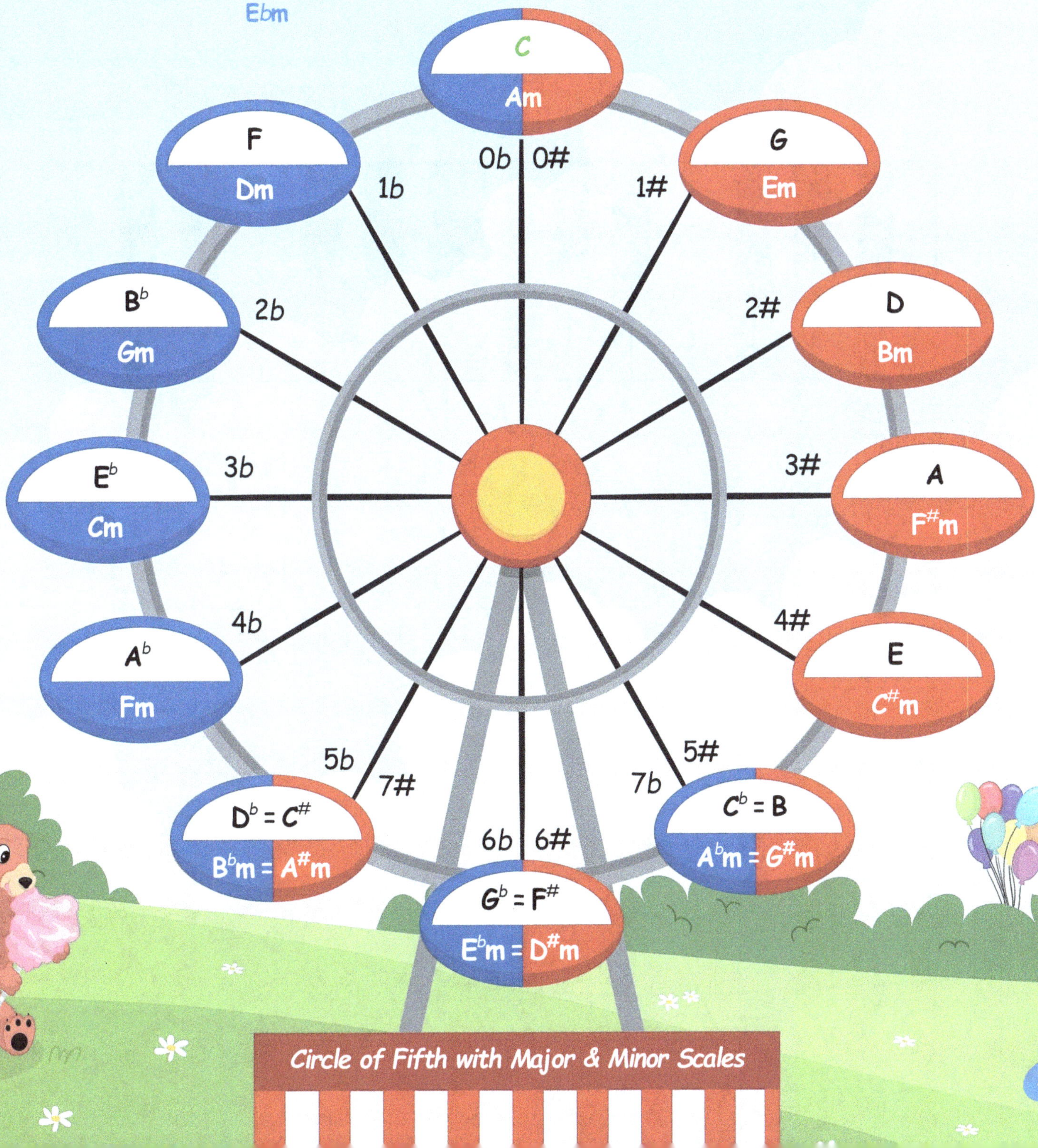

Circle of Fifth with Major & Minor Scales

MINOR SCALES WITH SHARPS

Minor Scales with Sharps

Minor scales with sharps are: Em, Bm, F#m, C#m, G#m, D#m, and A#m.

- Same as major scales, minor scales are built on the **fifth degree of the previous scale.**
- The primary minor scale is **A minor**, which is the **relative minor** of the **primary major scale, C major.**
- Every subsequent minor scale begins on the **upper P5** (the fifth degree) of the previous scale.
- With each new scale, a new **sharp** is added to the **second degree.**
- The sharps are added in the same order as in major scales: **F#, C#, G#, D#, A#, E#**, and **B#.**

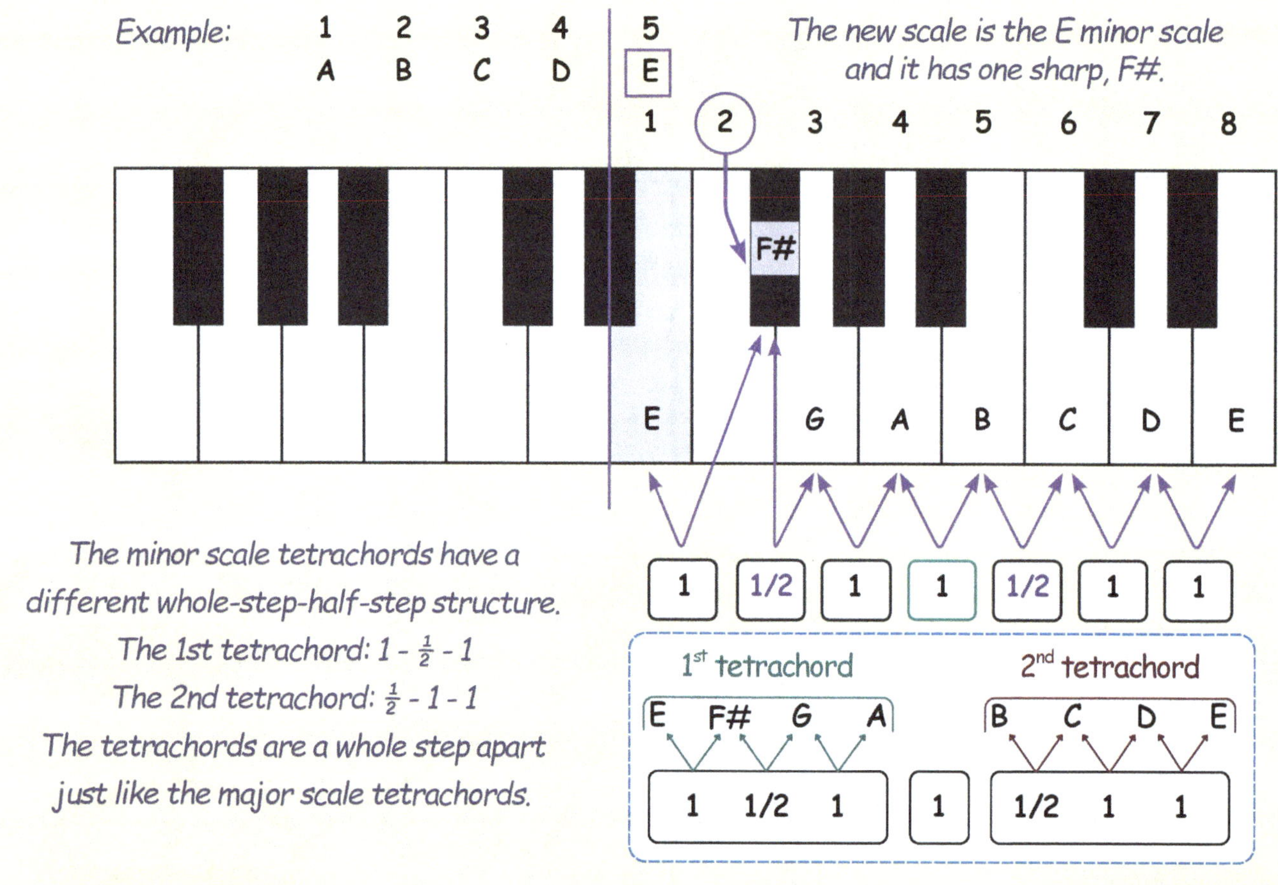

E Copy the sharps according to the example.
Fill the empty flags with the names of missing minor scales.

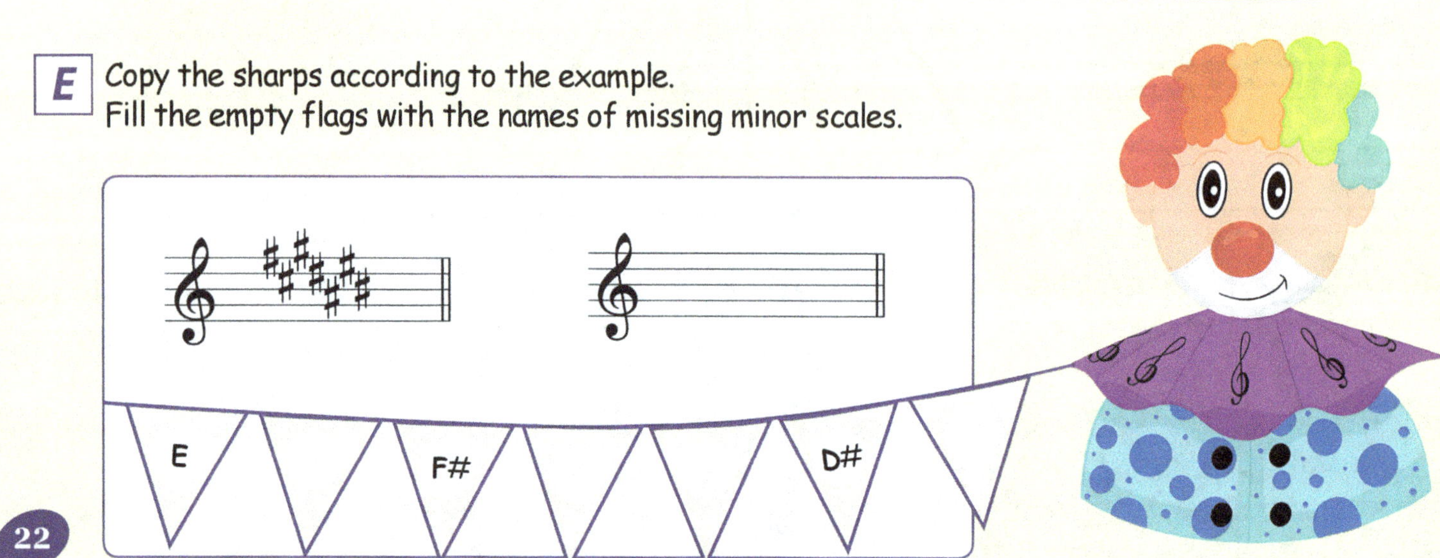

E MINOR – 1#

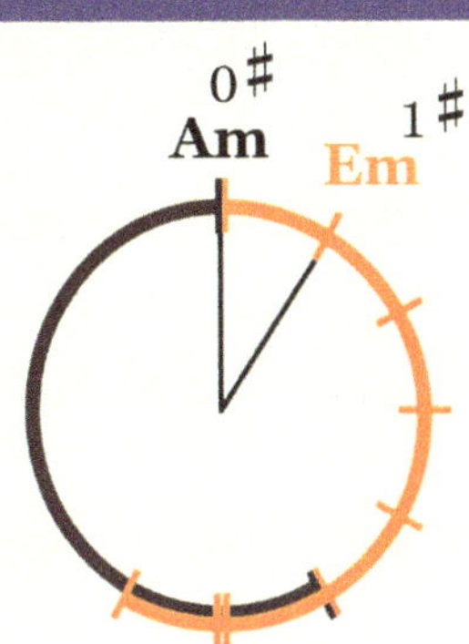

- Name: E minor – begins and ends on the note E.
- Key Signature: one sharp – F#.
- The minor scales with sharps: Em, Bm, F#m, C#m, G#m, D#m, A#m.

E natural minor

tonic fifth chord

E Bracket the half steps in the natural minor scale (above). Notate harmonic and melodic scales derived from the natural minor scale. Circle the raised (altered) notes in red.

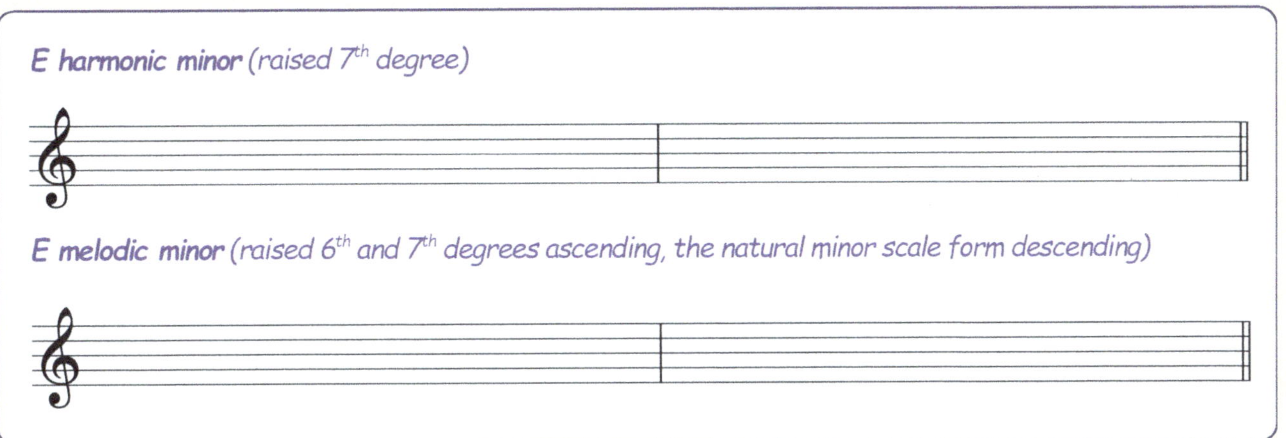

E The following beautiful Slovak folk song begins with a melodic minor fifth chord. Take some time to practice identifying it by ear. Review the ascending and descending fifth chords, and mark all instances present within the song, then notate both melodic fifth chords.

B MINOR - 2#

- Name: B minor – begins and ends on the note B.
- Key Signature: two sharps – F#, C#.
- The minor scales with sharps: Em, Bm, F#m, C#m, G#m, D#m, A#m.

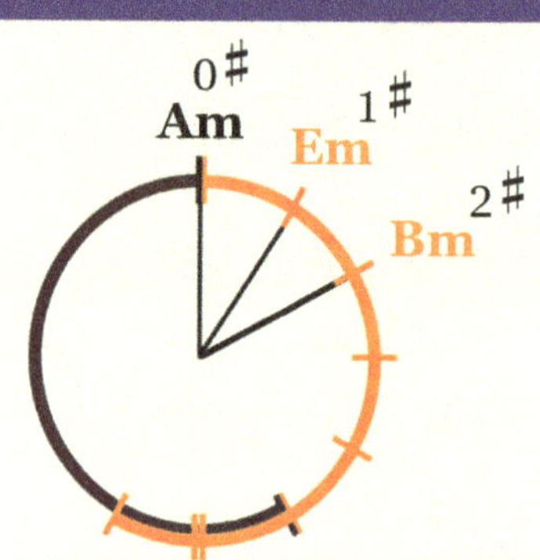

B natural minor

tonic fifth chord

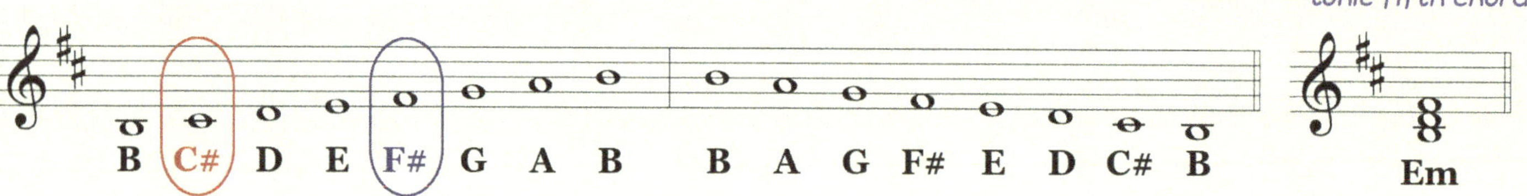

E Bracket the half steps in the natural minor scale (above).
Notate harmonic and melodic scales derived from the natural minor scale.

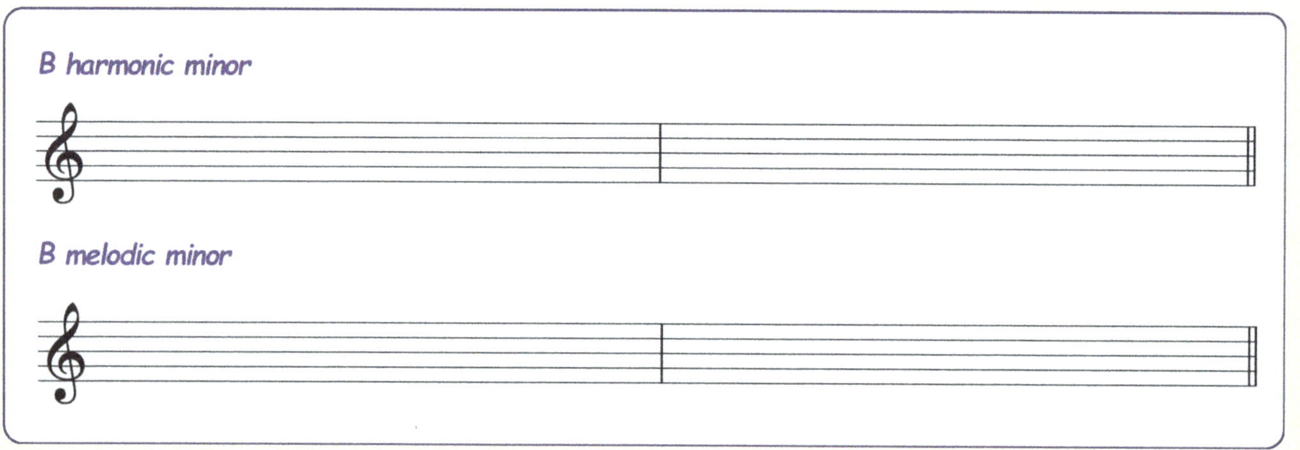

E The following song is in the key of B minor. In the third measure, while the melody is descending, there is a sharp in front of the note A = A#. What degree is the note A in B minor? ....
Circle all the notes A#. Figure out in which of the three minor scales (*natural, harmonic, or melodic*) is this song composed: ....

Clefi & Notelina's Songbook, pg. 85
Roads Are Guiding Us

F# MINOR - 3#

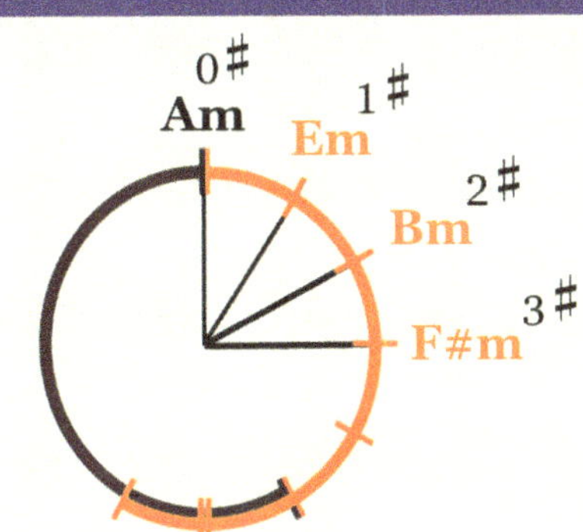

- Name: **F# minor** – begins and ends on the note **F#**.
- Key Signature: three sharps – F#, C#, G#.
- The minor scales with sharps: Em, Bm, **F#m**, C#m, G#m, D#m, A#m.

F# natural minor

tonic fifth chord

E | Notate harmonic and melodic scales derived from the natural minor scale.

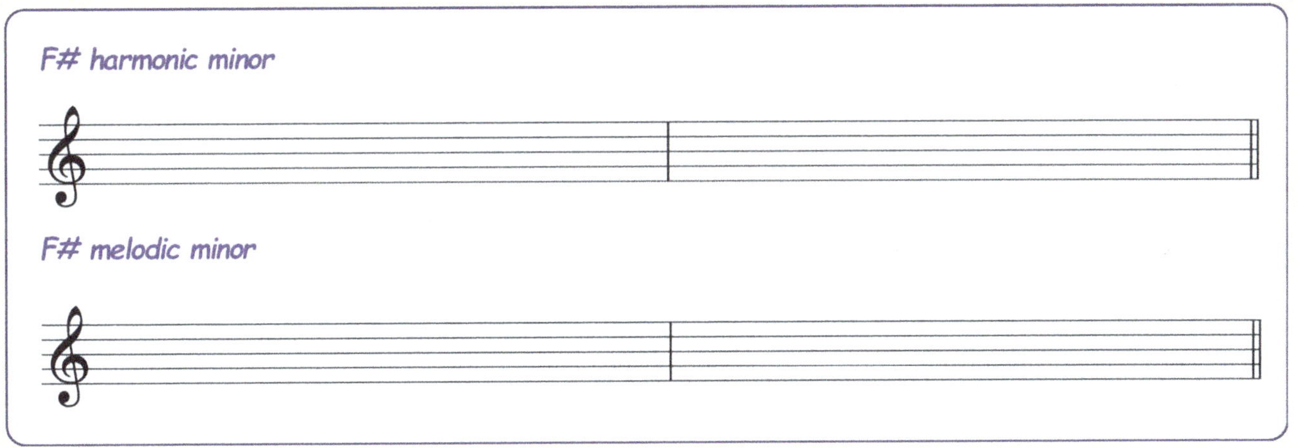

E | The song "Roads Are Guiding Us" from the previous page starts with characteristic progression towards the minor third. Transpose the opening section into assigned keys and bracket this progression in red. Notate the progression in minor and major keys according to the example.

C# MINOR - 4#

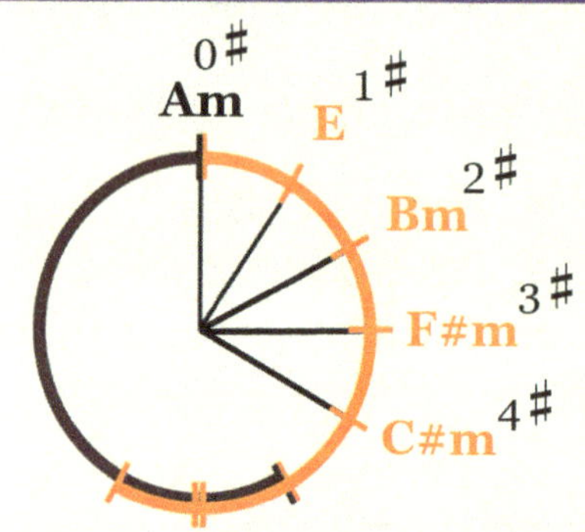

- Name: *C# minor* – begins and ends on the note *C#*
- Key Signature: four sharps – F#, C#, G#, D#
- The minor scales with sharps: Em, Bm, F#m, *C#m*, G#m, D#m, A#m.

C# natural minor

tonic fifth chord

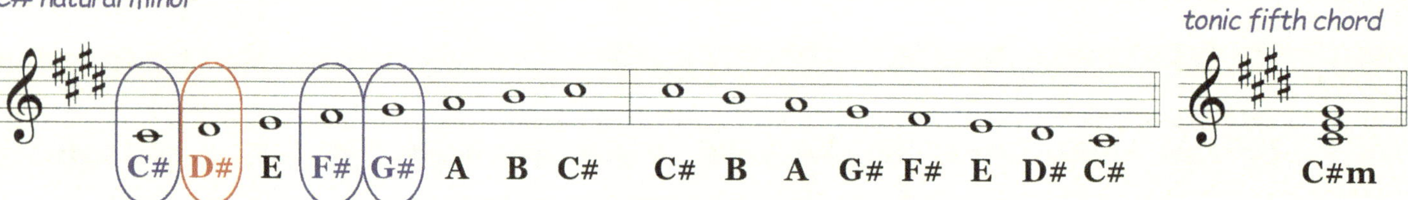

E Notate harmonic and melodic scales derived from the natural minor scale.

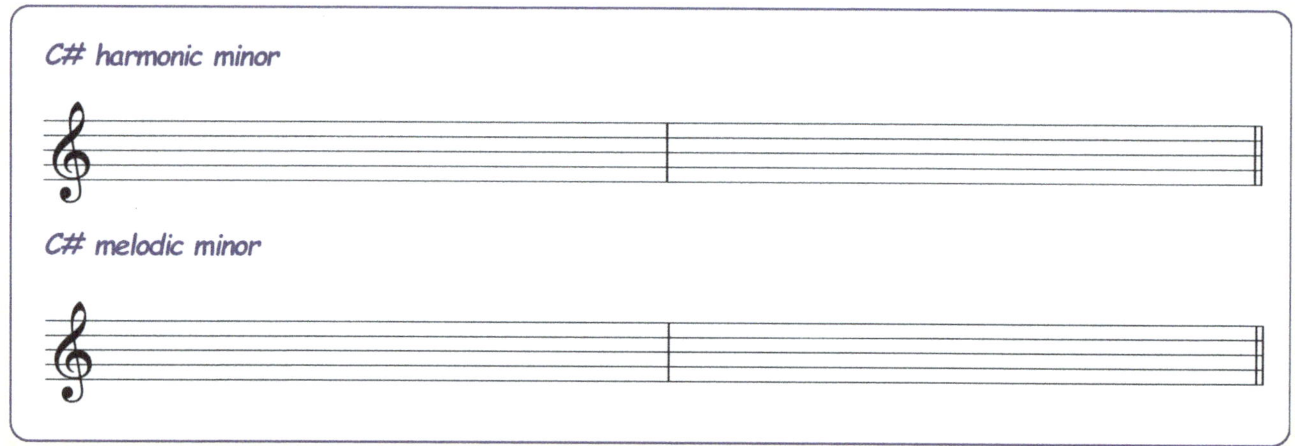

E Learn the following song starting with the descending melodic fifth chord. How many times it appears in the song? .... Bracket all occurrences of it. Notate ascending and descending melodic fifth chord in *C# minor*.

EXERCISES

E Fill in the table with the relative scales with sharps and their fifth chords.

major fifth chord	major scale	key sign.	minor scale	minor fifth chord
C-E-G	C major	0	A minor	A-C-E
		1#		
		2#		
		3#		
		4#		

E Analyze the song from page 26. Which scale degree does the song start on? ....
Transpose the first two measures of the song into the designated keys.

Clefi & Notelina's Songbook, pg. 87

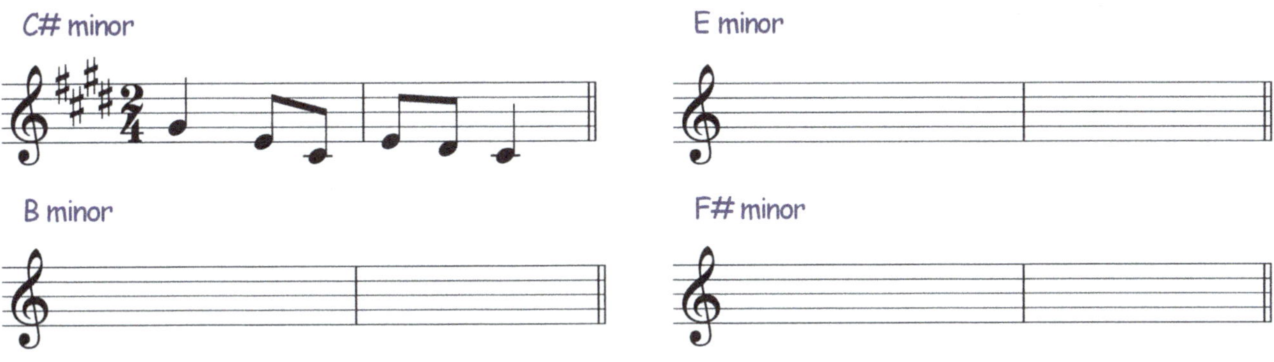

E Link the cups with their corresponding straws.

HARMONIC FUNCTIONS

Harmonic analysis is the study of the chord structure and their relationships within a musical composition.

Harmonic functions are chords built on the individual scale degrees and labeled according to their relationship the tonic, the root tone of a scale.

The fifth chords built on the foundational degrees are:

T = tonic fifth chords - built on the 1st degree
S = subdominant fifth chords - built on the 4th degree
D = dominant fifth chords - built on the 5th degree

Major Scale Foundational Harmonic Functions
Most simple songs can be accompanied using the foundational degrees of the scale (T, S, D).
The labels T, S, and D are applicable to any key.
Typically, these songs begin with the tonic fifth chord.

In most songbooks, the chord symbols corresponding to the song's key are placed above the melody. As you can see in both our songbooks, as well.

Example in C major:

E Review the song "Little Cuckoo Bird" in the key of C major. Fill the function symbols into the frames according to the chords labels . Transpose the song section into D major including the accompaniment chord progression symbols (follow the function symbols for help).

Clefi & Notelina's Songbook, pg. 54   *"Clefi's Music Notebook 1" page 29*

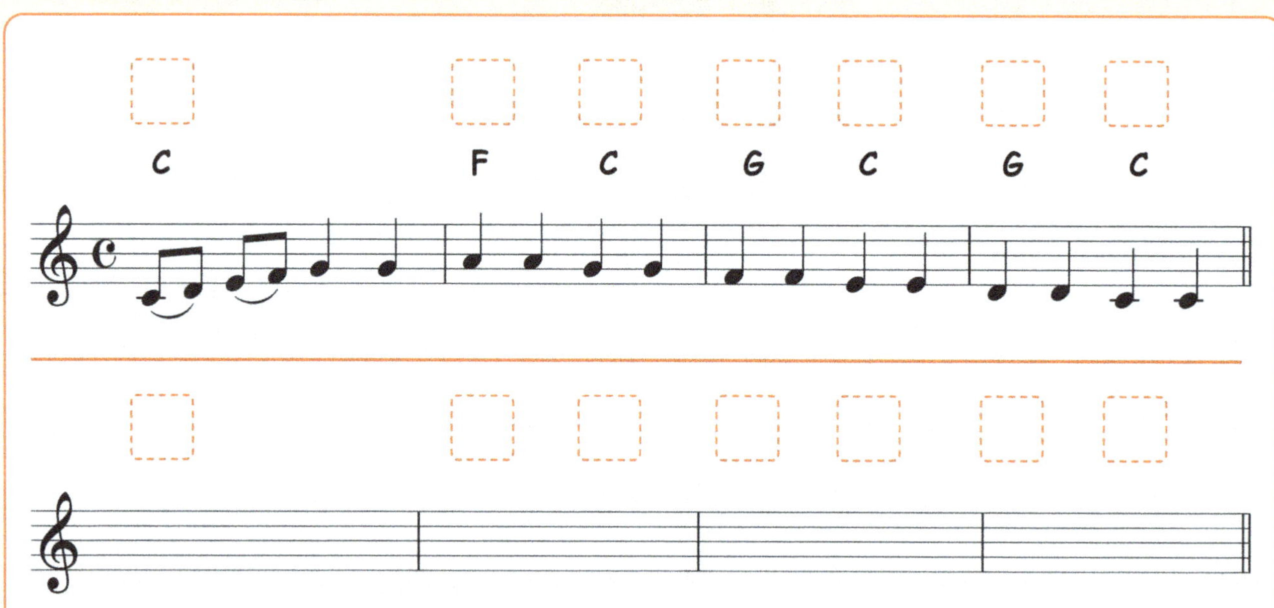

Fundamental Harmonic Functions in Minor Scales

The basic harmonic functions in minor scales are formed the same way as in major.
They built the **fifth chords on the 1st, 4th, and 5th degrees**.
We always use the **notes of the specific scale or its version** to create their structure.

Example in C major:

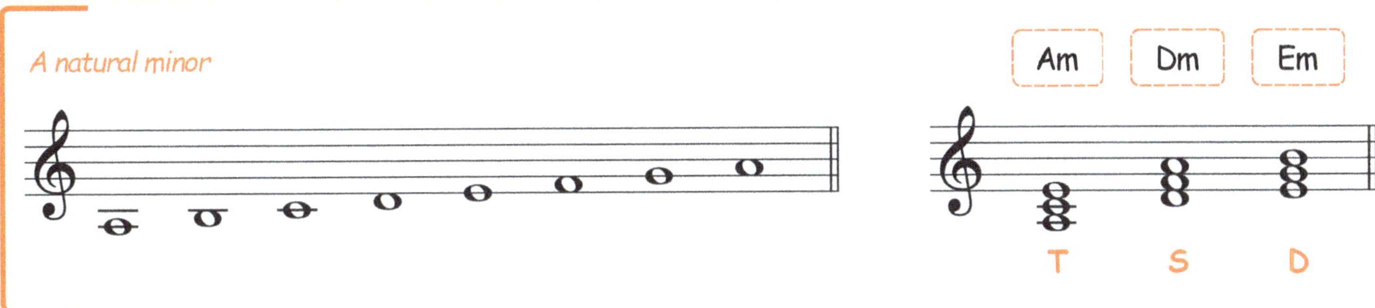

A natural minor

Fundamental Harmonic Functions in Derived Minor Scales

Given that there are three variations of a minor scale, the **chords created** to support melodies derived from each **must align with the respective scale.** Altered (raised) notes in harmonic and melodic scales are essential and must be used in the accompanying harmonic functions.

major dominant

A harmonic minor

major subdominant and dominant

A melodic minor - ascending

A melodic minor - descending

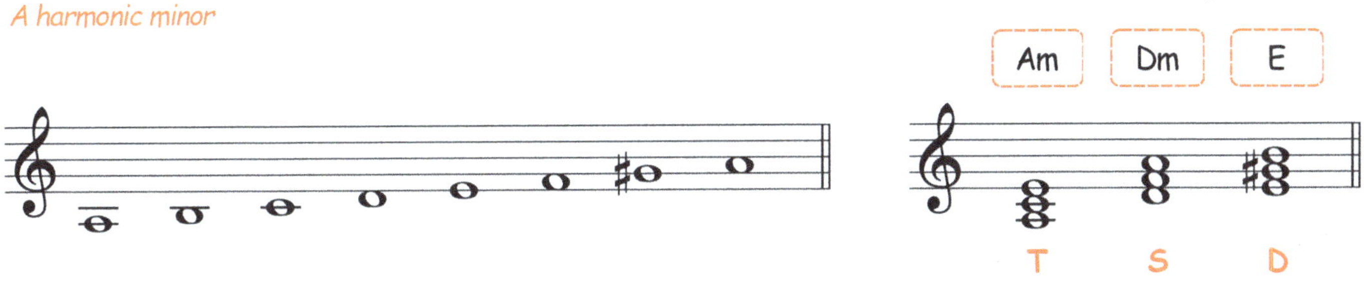

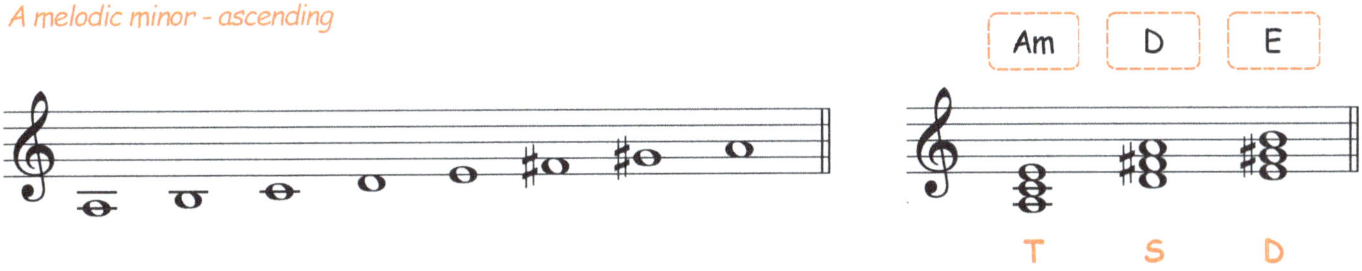

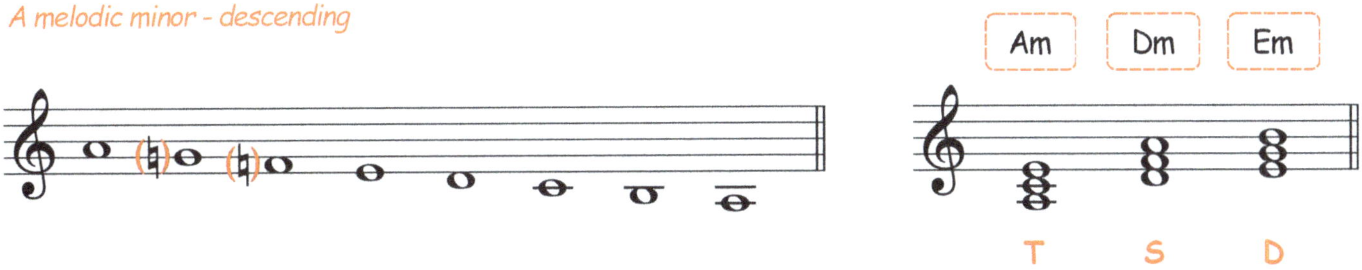

a descending melodic scale is essentially natural minor, the chords are also minor

Minor Scales with Flats

Minor scales with sharps are: **Dm**, **Gm**, **Cm**, **Fm**, **Bbm**, **Ebm**, and **Abm**.

- Same as major scales, minor scales with flats are built on the lower P5 or its inversion the upper P4 (the fourth degree). It's common to use the ascending progression.
- The primary minor scale is **A minor**, which has no key signature.
- Every minor scale begins on the **lower P5** or the **upper P4** of the previous scale.
- With each new scale, a **flat is added to the sixth degree**.
- The flats are added in the same order as in major scales: **Bb**, **Eb**, **Ab**, **Db**, **Gb**, **Cb**, and **Fb**.

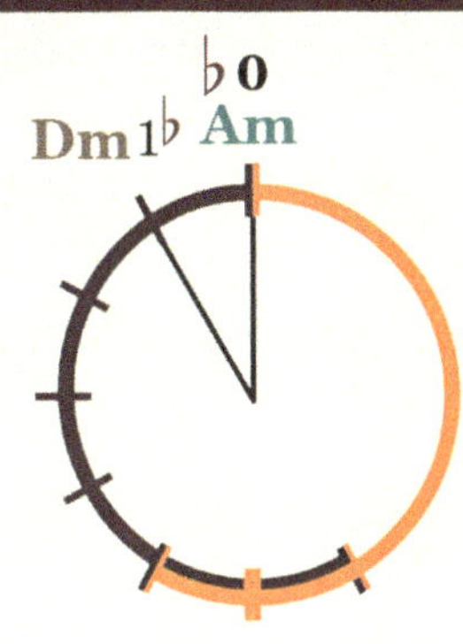

- Name: D minor – begins and ends on the note D.
- Key Signature: one flat – B♭
- The minor scales with flats: Dm, Gm, Cm, Fm, B♭m, E♭m, A♭m.

D natural minor

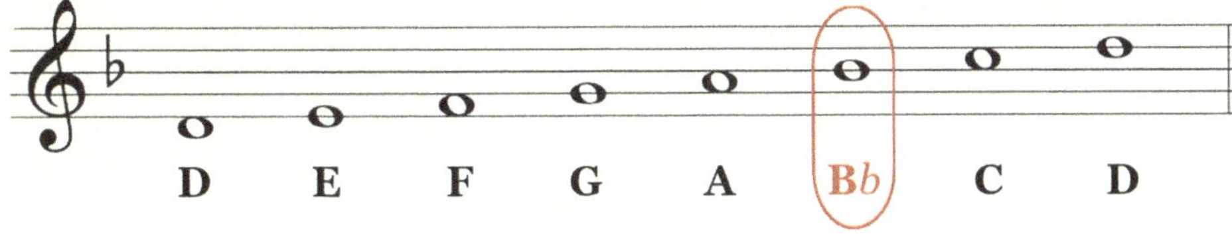

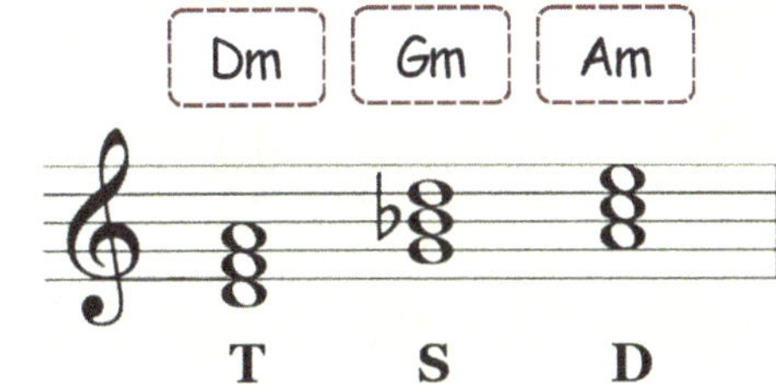

Derived Minor Scales

- If a note that should be raised while creating a harmonic or melodic scale has been **lowered by the key signature**, it must be altered (raised) using a **natural sign**.
- The **altered (raised) notes** within a scale remain applicable even for **harmonic functions chords**.

Major chords with a major third at the bottom are labeled with **uppercase letters** (C, D, etc.).
Minor chords with a minor third at the bottom are labeled using **uppercase letter followed by a lowercase "m"** (Cm, Dm, etc.).

E Name the notes of the melodic minor scale. Circle the raised note in red. Write the chord names indicating the harmonic function for both the ascending and descending melodic minor scales. Color the boxes with major chords in yellow.

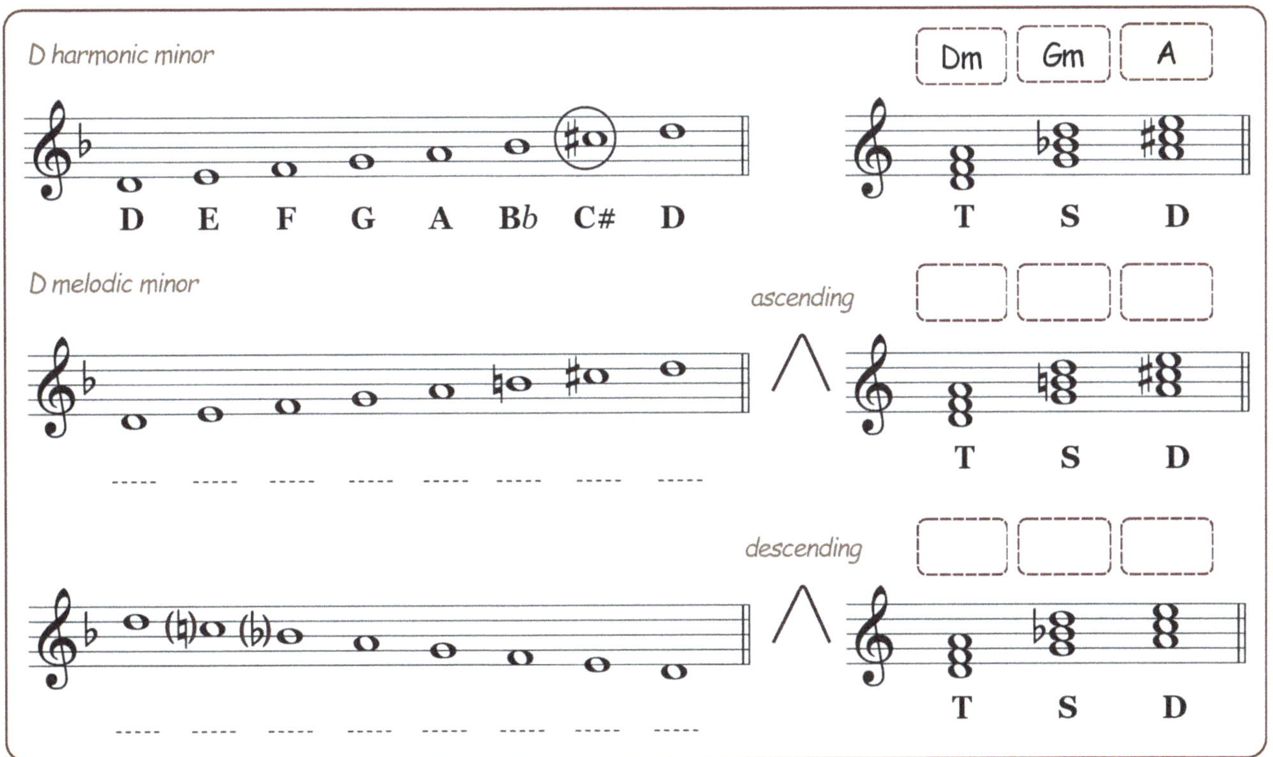

G MINOR - 2♭

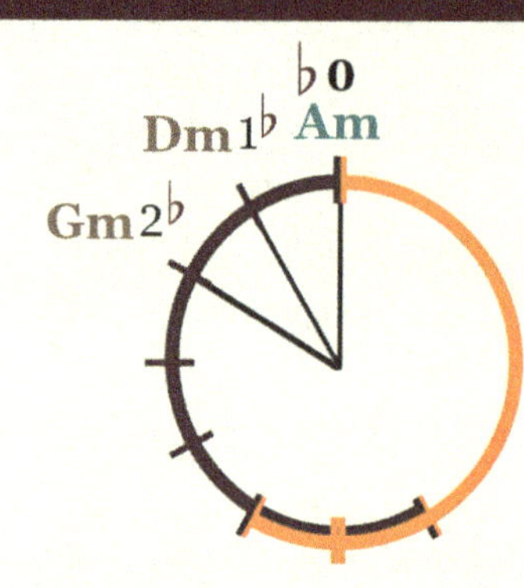

- Name: *G minor* – begins and ends on the note *G*.
- Key Signature: two flats - B♭, E♭.
- The minor scales with flats: Dm, *Gm*, Cm, Fm, B♭m, E♭m, A♭m.

D natural minor

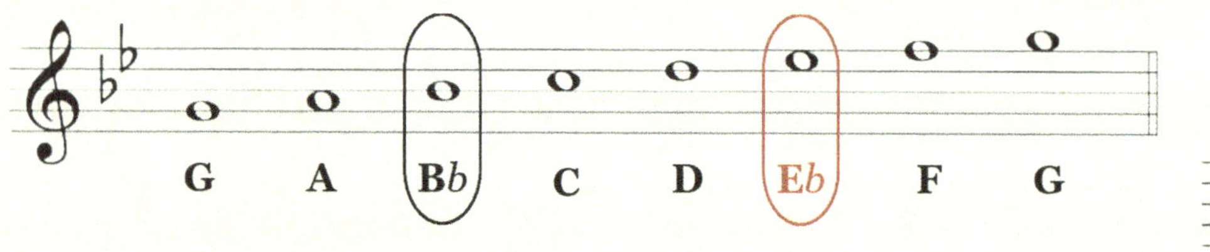

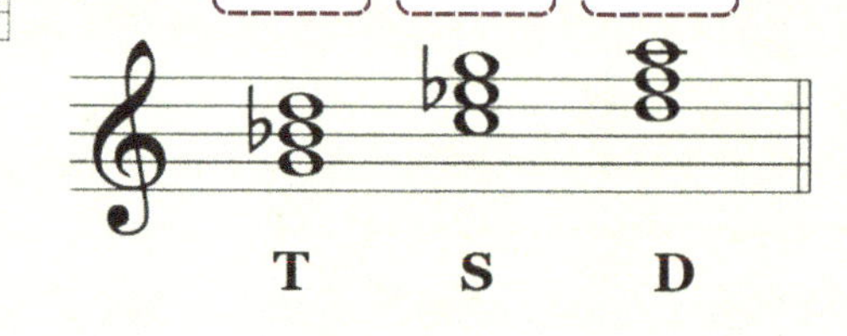

E Notate the harmonic and melodic G minor scale. Circle the raised notes. Notate the basic harmonic function for each scale, and name them in the boxes. The ones with major chords color yellow.

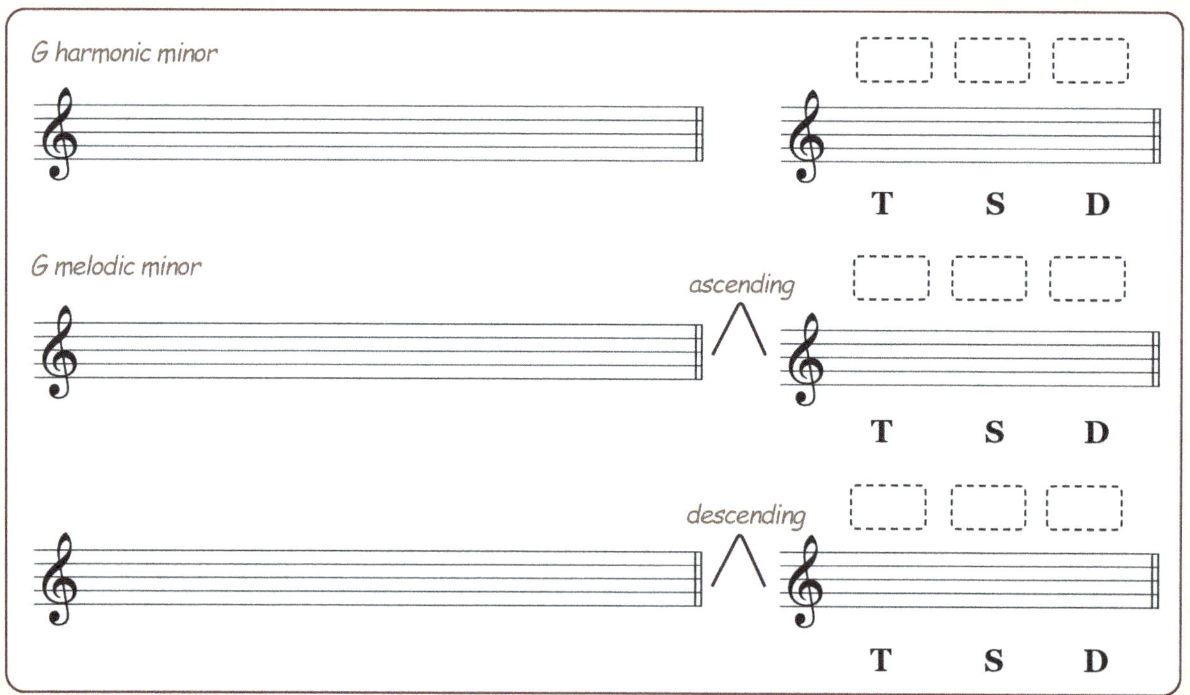

E Transpose the opening section of the song "Have You Forgotten Me?" into G minor. The song is composed in the harmonic minor mode. Pay close attention and color the boxes with major chords.

Clefi & Notelina's Songbook, pg. 87

C MINOR - 3♭

- Name: *C minor* – begins and ends on the note *C*.
- Key Signature: three flats – Bb, Eb, Ab.
- The minor scales with flats: Dm, Gm, **Cm**, Fm, Bbm, Ebm, Abm.

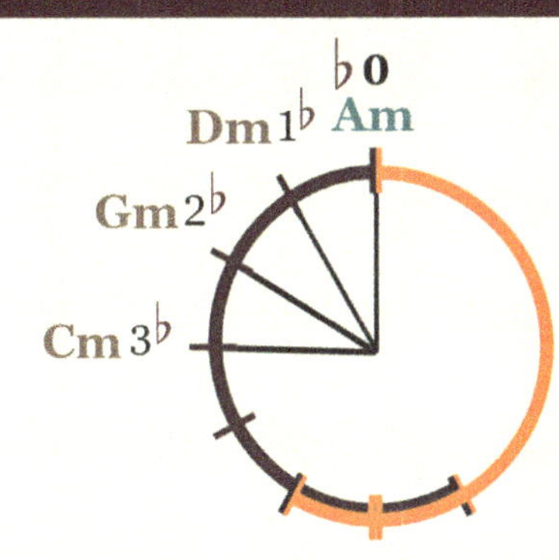

C natural minor

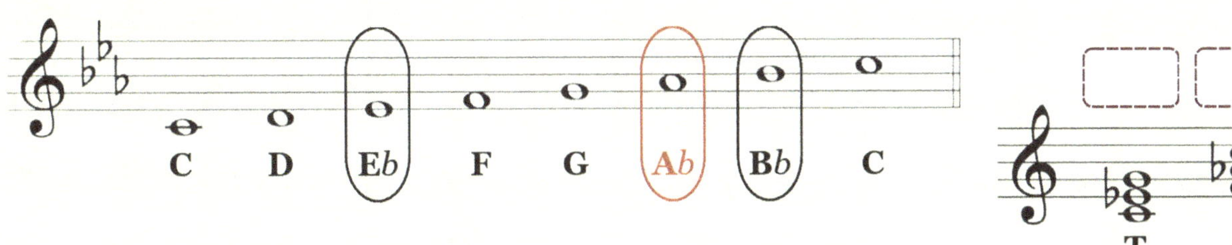

E   Notate the harmonic and melodic C minor scale. Circle the raised notes. Notate the basic harmonic function for each scale, and name them in the boxes. The ones with major chords color yellow.

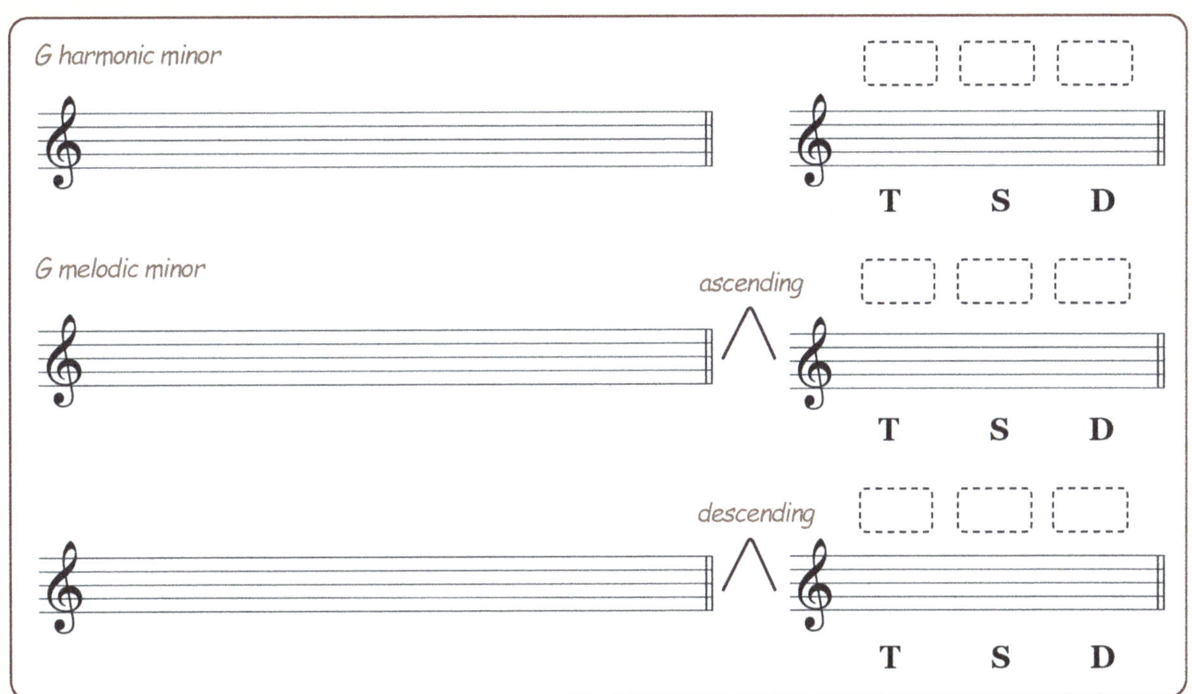

E   Observing the chord labels, determine the minor key and the mode of the new song: ....
Write the harmonic function symbols above the boxes with chord names.

Clefi & Notelina's Songbook, pg. 88
My, Love, You Cruel Love

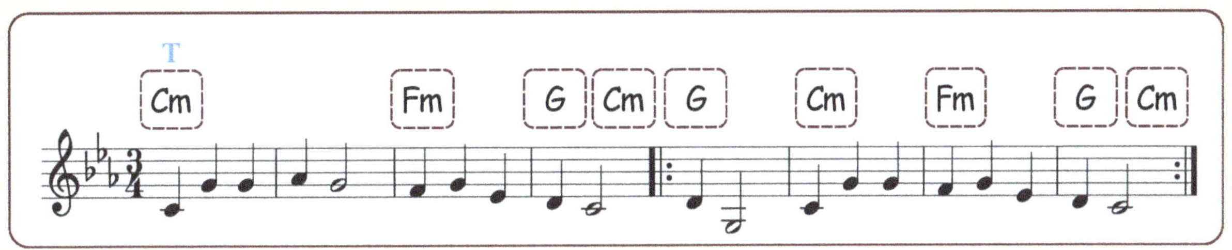

- Name: **F minor** – begins and ends on the note **F**.
- Key Signature: four flats - B♭, E♭, A♭, D♭.
- The minor scales with flats: Dm, Gm, Cm, **Fm**, B♭m, E♭m, A♭m.

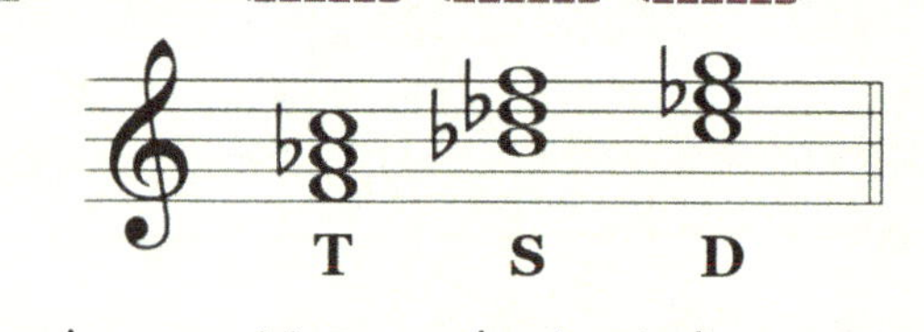

F natural minor

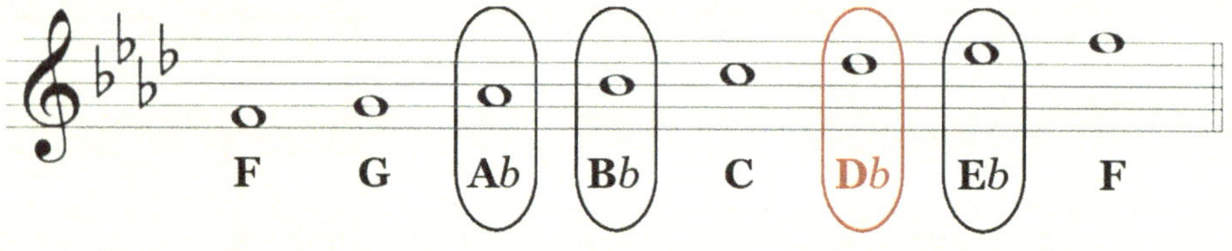

E Notate the harmonic and melodic F minor scale. Circle the raised notes. Notate the basic harmonic function for each scale, and name them in the boxes. The ones with major chords color yellow.

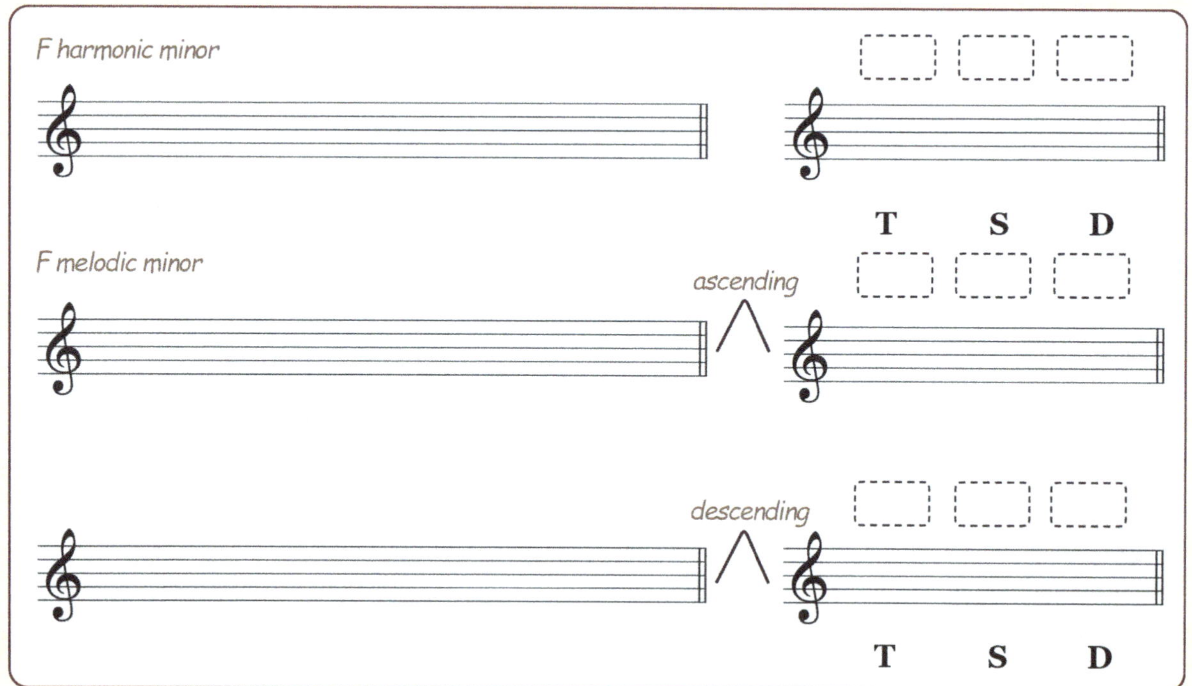

E Observing the chord labels, determine the minor key and the mode of the song: ....
Write the harmonic function symbols above the boxes with chord names.

Clefi & Notelina's Songbook, pg. 81
Good Night, My Sweet Love

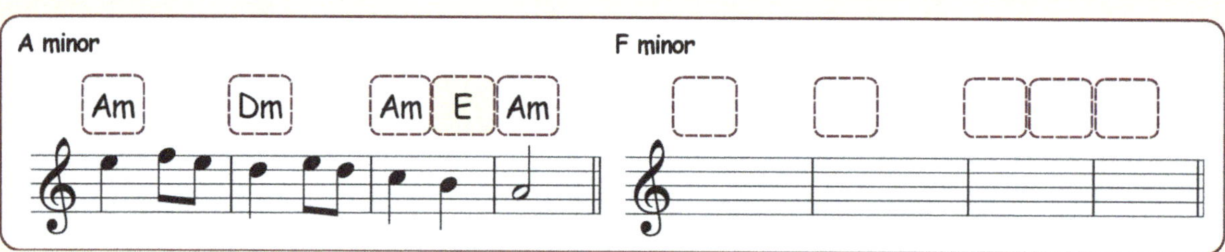

REVIEW

MAJOR & MINOR SCALES

- **Relative major and minor scales** share the key signature.
- **Parallel major and minor scales** share the same tonic (naming) note.

E Fill in the table.

| PARALLEL minor scale | | | PARALLEL SCALES | | | PARALLEL major scale |
key sign.	name ⟷	MAJOR	key sign.	MINOR ⟷	name	key sign.
3b	C minor	C major	b0#	A minor	A major	3#
			1#			
			2#			
			3#			
			4#			
			1b			
			2b			
			3b			
			4b			

CHROMATIC SCALE

In Western music, there are just 12 pitch-specific tones. This is evident on a keyboard, which has 7 white and 5 black keys, totaling 12. When we arrange these tones in a row, we get the so-called chromatic scale. This scale can be built from any note (C, C#, D, D#, E...).

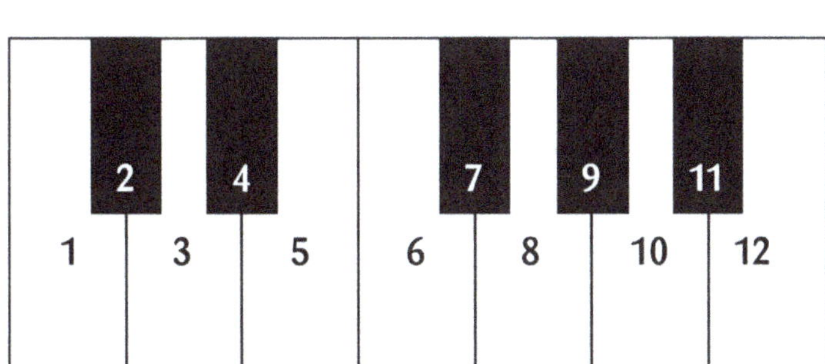

E Write the names of the tones in the chromatic scale by observing the keyboard. Use sharps only when necessary.

2/2, 3/2, 6/4, & 9/8 MEASURES

SIMPLE MEASURE

Simple measures are all **two-** and **three-beat measures**.
Simple measures have only **one heavy beat**, which mostly falls
on the downbeat.

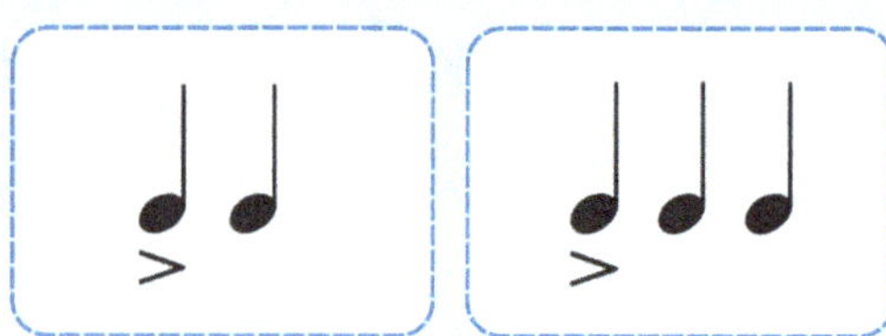

COMBINED MEASURES

Combined measures are **multi-beat measures** that can be easily **divided into tow or
more simple measures**. The combined measure has the **main heavy beat** on the first
beat - **the downbeat** - and one or more **secondary heavy beats**.

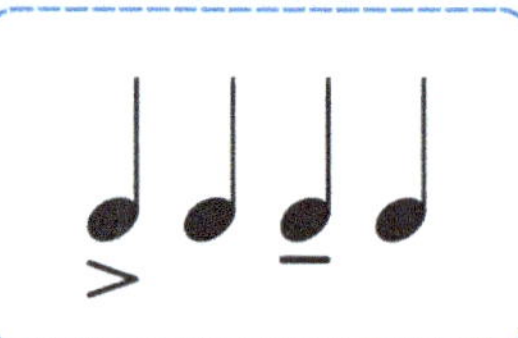

Counting the beats in a measure depends on the **basic unit of the time signature**. The basic unit is the
beat, so we count it as *"one"* regardless of the note value (quarter, half, eighth note...).

Basic measures we encountered so far are:
simple - 2/4 and 3/4
combined - 4/4 and 6/8

Additional common measures included:
simple - 2/2, 3/2, or 3/8
combined - 9/8 or 6/4

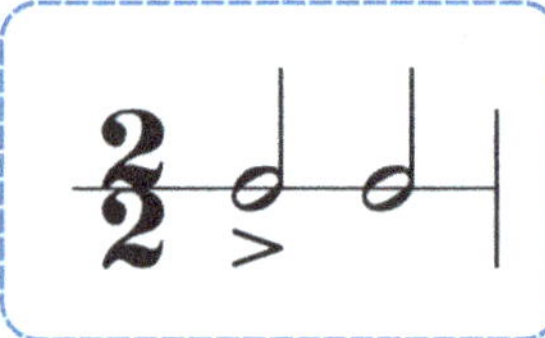

Two-Two Measure - **Cut Time**
The basic unit is a **half note**.
Another symbol for this meter is ₵ .
There are two **beats** in this measure.
The accent falls on the **downbeat**.

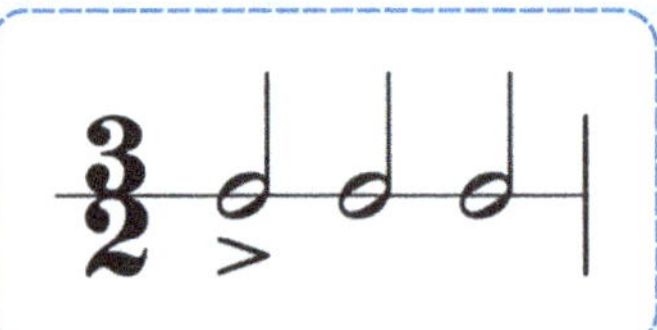

Three-Two Measure
The basic unit is a **half note**.
There are **three beats** in this measure.
The accent falls on the **downbeat**.

E The 3/2 meter or time signature can be found in one of Smetana's symphonic poems, "Tábor."
Mark the accents. Clap the rhythm while counting out loud.

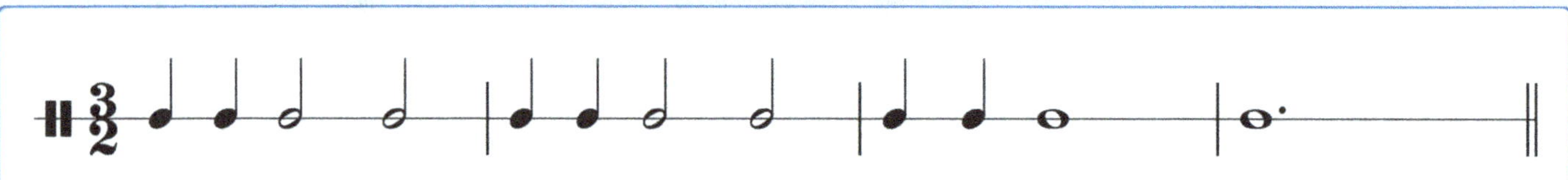

Three-Eight Measure

The basic unit is an **eighth note**.
There are **three beats** in this measure.
The accent falls on the **downbeat**.

Nine-Eight Measure

The basic unit is an **eighth note**.
There are **nine beats** in this measure.
The main accent falls on the **downbeat**.
Two secondary accents fall on the 4th and 7th beats.

E The 3/2 meter or time signature can be found in one of Smetana's symphonic poems, "Tábor."
Mark the accents. Clap the rhythm while counting out loud.

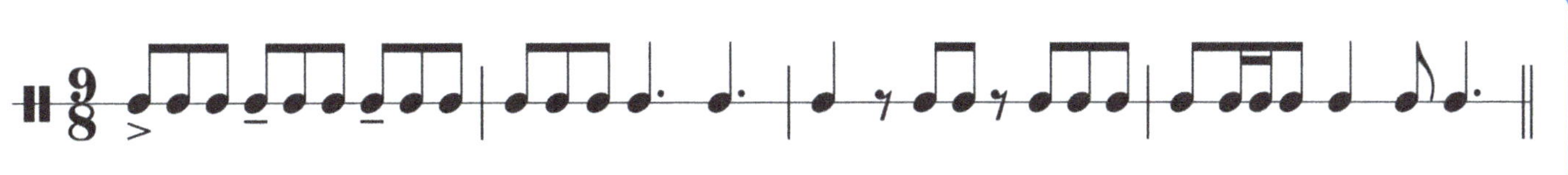

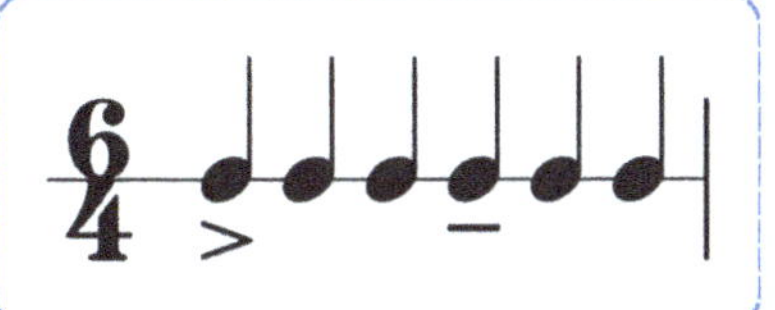 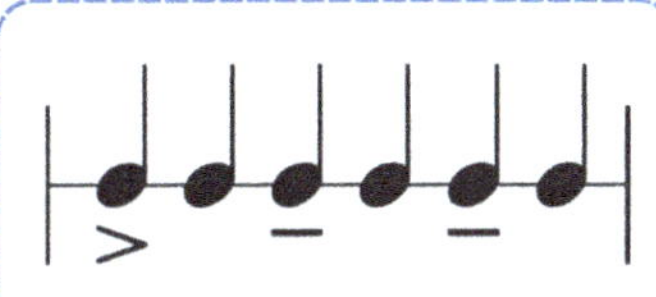

Six-Four Measure

The basic unit is a **quarter note**.
There are **six beats** in this measure.
The accent falls on the **downbeat**.
The secondary accent(s) may fall either on
the 4th or on the 3rd and 5th beats.

A 6/4 measure can be split into **two 3/4 measures** or **three 2/4 measures**.
When divided into **two 3/4 parts**, accents fall on the first and fourth beats, creating a **compound meter**.
Compound meter refers to any time signature where a measure is split into multiple accents, each aligned
with the first of three notes - 9/8 (*three groups of three eighth notes*), 6/8, 12/8, 6/4 and so on.

E The aria lullaby "Little White Dove" from Smetana's opera *The Kiss* is composed in a 6/4 meter.
In this instance, the measure consists of six beats that can be divided into two 3/4 measures,
classifying it as a compound meter. Mark all the main accents in the excerpt below.

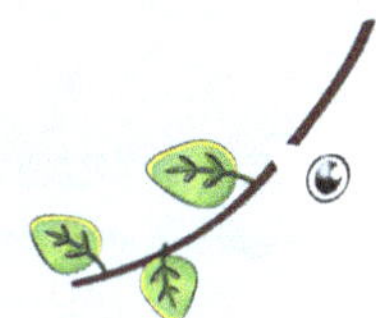

RHYTHMIC EXERCISES

 Learn the rhythmic exercises using a pencil or a wooden stick. Tap out the rhythm, and then add your other hand to emphasize the downbeats.

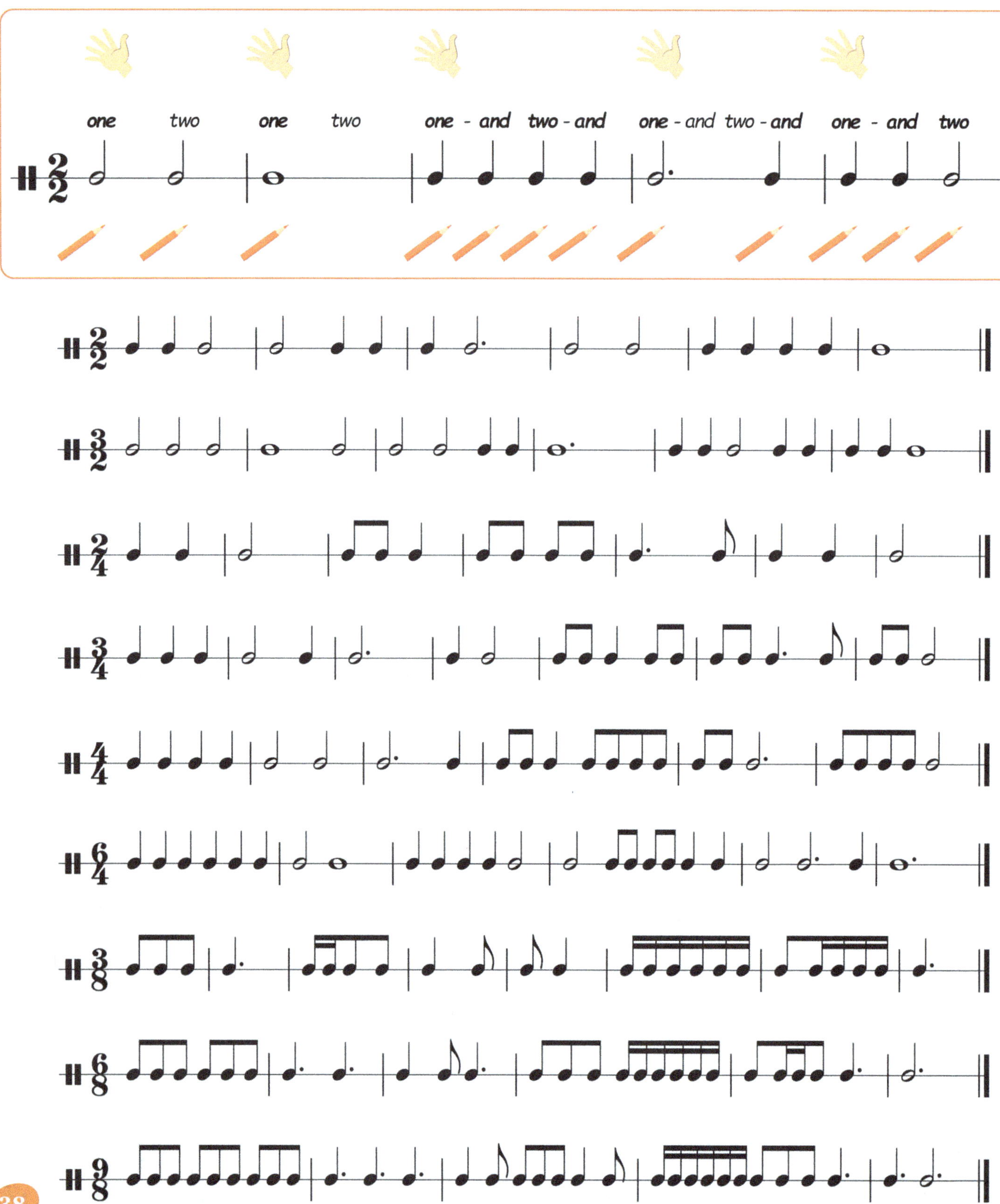

E Write the notes according to the time signatures. Mark primary and secondary accents. Tap or clap out the rhythms. Color the boxes: use red for simple and yellow for combined measures. Mark the measures with the compound meter.

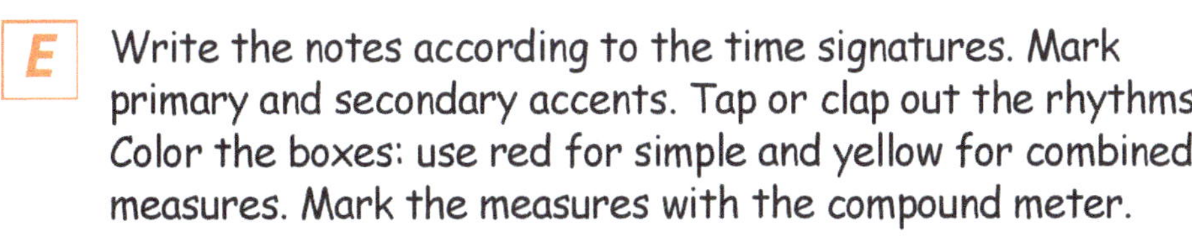

E How many notes can fit into these measures? Write the corresponding numbers in the boxes next to the time signatures.

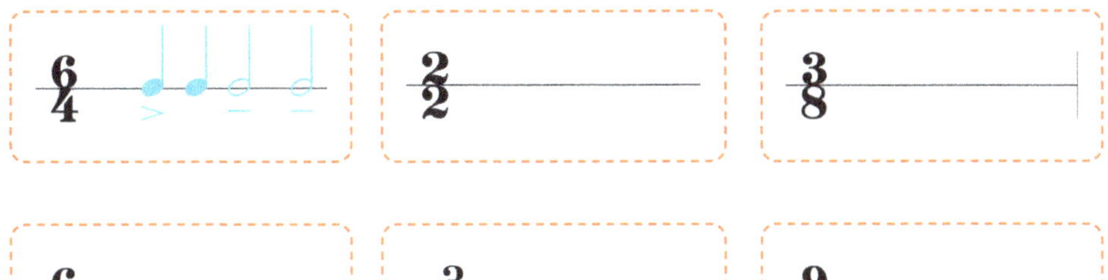

E Fill in the bar lines according to the meters and mark all main and secondary accents. Draw the notes that represents the fundamental unit of the time signature.

MUSIC TERMINOLOGY

Music is typically divided into two primary categories: **vocal** and **instrumental**.
Vocal music is created for the human voice or multiple voices, often referred to simply as vocals.
Instrumental music is performed using one or more musical instruments.

Music can also be categorized according to the number of musicians performing as:

- **Solo Music**: Designed for a single voice or instrument, with or without vocal or instrumental accompaniment.
- **Chamber Music**: Composed for small groups of singers and/or instrumentalists, including ensembles like duos (2), trios (3), quartets (4), nonets (9), but generally no more than 11 members
- **Choir or Choral Music**: Intended for larger vocal ensembles and choirs.
- **Orchestral Music**: Instrumental compositions for larger ensembles, such as string chamber orchestras, mixed chamber or solo orchestras, symphony orchestras, or philharmonic orchestras.

Interpretation

Interpretation refers to the manner in which a musical composition is performed, shaped by various factors such as style, historical period, the composer's intentions, the performer's technical skill, personal taste, musical perspective, and emotional state. Performers are often referred to as "interpreters."

Conductor

A **conductor** is a performing artist leading a larger instrumental or combined ensemble in rehearsals and public performances.
A conductor of a large vocal ensemble is called a **choir director**.

Score

A **score** is a printed or digital document that displays the complete musical notation for all vocal and instrumental parts in a composition involving two or more performers. While all musicians use a score during rehearsal and study, only a conductor uses it during a public performance.
A **part** is a printed or digital notation of a single voice or instrumental line.

Intonation

Intonation refers to singing or playing **in tune** - that is, producing clean, precise pitch and tone color. Singing or playing in any ensemble requires accurate intonation and a strong sense of rhythm.
Concert pitch is a reference tone provided to all musicians prior to ensemble rehearsals or performances to ensure that all instruments are uniformly tuned. The most commonly used concert pitch is **concert A (A4)**.

CERTIFICATE

OF COMPLETION

This certificate is presented to:

For successfully completing

Clefi's Music Notebook 3

music education teacher

Clefi's and Notelina's
Little American-British-International Music Dictionary

Music is a universal language; that is true. However, every nation uses its own beautiful tongue to describe and teach music. Clefi is originally Klíček, a little Czech boy who guides children through the fundamentals of music theory using the Czech language and music terminology. His American twin brother Clefi had to translate and adapt the text so English-speaking children could enjoy the journey. However, not all English-speaking musicians use the same music terms. Therefore, Clefi created this little American-British Music Dictionary of music terms used in this book to accommodate our British English-speaking music friends.

Octaves

Zero octave	Sub-contra octave
First octave	Contra octave
Second octave	Great octave
Thirds octave	Small octave
Fourth (middle) octave	One-line octave
Fifth octave	Two-line octave
Sixth octave	Three-line octave
Seventh octave	Four-line octave

Notes

C1-B1	C, *(contra)* - B, *(contra)*
C2-B2	C *(great)* - B *(great)*
C3-B3	c *(small)* - b *(small)*
C4-B4 (middle)	c'-b' *(one-line c - 1 line b)*
C5-B5	c''-b'' *(two-line c - 2 line b)*
C6-B6	c'''-b''' *(three-line c - 3 line b)*
C7-B7	Cc''''-b'''' *(four-line c - 4 line b)*

General Music Terms

Staff *(Staffs)*	Stave *(Staves)*
Grand staff	Great stave
Measure, measure line	Bar, Barline
Fermata	Pause, Hold

Note Distances

Whole step	Tone
Half step	Semitone

Note Values

Double whole note *(rest)*	Breve *(rest)*
Whole note *(rest)*	Semibreve *(rest)*
Half note *(rest)*	Minim *(rest)*
Quarter note *(rest)*	Crotchet *(rest)*
Eighth note *(rest)*	Quaver *(rest)*
Sixteenth note *(rest)*	Semiquaver *(rest)*
Thirty-second note *(rest)*	Demisemiquaver *(rest)*
Sixty-fourth note *(rest)*	Hemidemisemiquaver *(rest)*

Across continental Europe, the rich musical tradition has led most countries to adopt Italian names for numerous musical symbols and terms, particularly for intervals. While we could provide a detailed comparison with country-specific translations and adaptations, we believe it's more effective to engage your musical intuition. Therefore, we invite you to explore the beauty and expressiveness of music by focusing solely on the Italian names of the most commonly used intervals. Embrace this journey and let your imagination resonate whenever you encounter a musical friend from another country!.

Unison .... Prima
Second .... Seconda
Third .... Terza
Fourth .... Quarta
Fifth .... Quinta
Sixth .... Sesta
Seventh .... Settima
Octave .... Ottava
Ninth .... Nona
Tenth .... Decima
Eleventh .... Undicesima
Twelfth .... Dodicesima

One Final Question

What musical terms, names comes to your mind when you look at the pictures below? in the pictures below? Write them in the box.

$$\text{♩} = 60$$

Answer Key to Clefi's Little Crossword Review

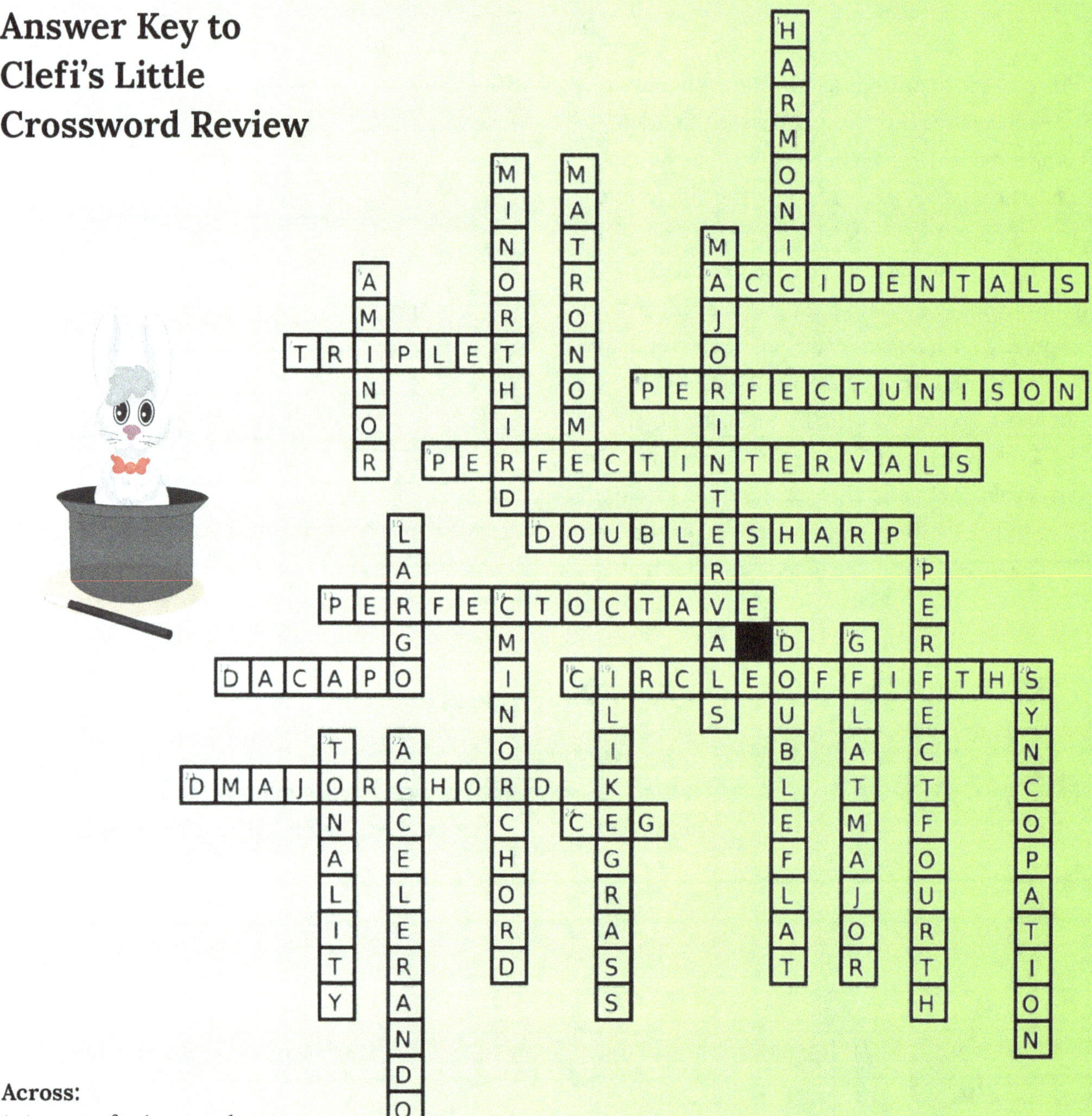

Across:

1. A type of minor scale.

2. m3.

3. A device indicating various tempos.

4. Second, third, sixth, and seventh.

5. The primary minor scale.

10. A broad, slow tempo marking.

12. The inverted perfect fifth.

14. Cm is a chord symbol for…

15. A symbol lowering a note by two half steps.

16. A major scale with six flats.

19. The name of the song starting with m2.

20. An irregular rhythmic pattern.

21. A mode.

22 A tempo marking for speeding up.

Down:

6. Symbols used to alter primary tones.

7. A three-note subdivision of a beat.

8. P1.

9. Unison, fourth, fifth, and octave.

11. A symbol raising a note by two half steps.

13. P8.

17. "Back to the beginning."

18. A diagram for the progression of all major and minor scales..

23. D is a chord symbol for…

24. C major tonic fifth chord.

Join Clefi's musical family!
Clefi invites you to visit his dedicated webpage and explore the enchanting musical world of Dr. Eva's New Music Education School Series. Learn more about the author and about the content of every volume of the series, dive into engaging materials, find answers to all the exercises, discover more songs, and further deepen your love and understanding of music and music education. Come make music with us!

www.bumblebeenotes.com/clefis-musical-world

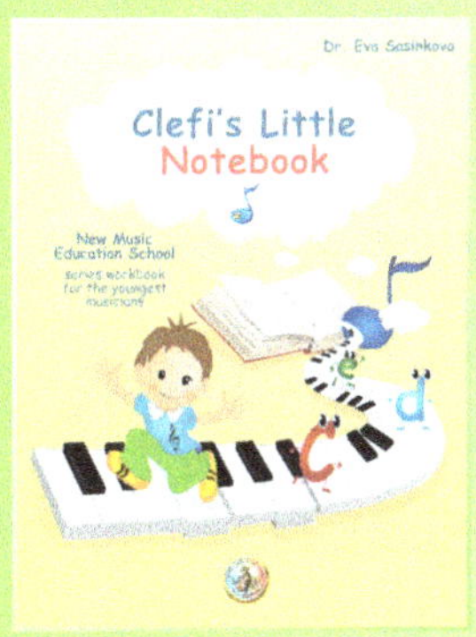

www.bumblebeenotes.com/music-publishing